EDITED BY MONTE BEAUCHAMP

THE LIFE AND TIMES OF R. CRUMB:
COMMENTS FROM CONTEMPORARIES

ST. MARTIN'S GRIFFIN ❧ NEW YORK

Foreword copyright ©1998 by Matt Groening
Front cover illustration ©1998 Drew Friedman

Interior designed by Monte Beauchamp
St. Martin's Press editor: Corin See

Library of Congress Cataloging-in-Publication Data

The Life and Times of R. Crumb/[edited by] Monte Beauchamp.
p. cm.
ISBN 0-312-19571-0
1. Crumb, R. 2. Cartoonists–United States–Biography.
I. Beauchamp, Monte.
NC1429.C83L54 1998
741.5′ 092–dc21
[B]   98-18842
                         CIP

First St. Martin's Griffin Edition: November 1998

10 9 8 7 6 5 4 3 2 1

In memory of Charles Addams and Dr. Seuss,
the first artists to spark my imagination.

R. CRUMB ILLUSTRATIONS:

Page i: "Keep On Truckin'...," *Zap* #1, ©1967 R. Crumb, originally published by Apex Novelties.

Page iii: "Mr. Natural Gets the Bum's Rush," *The East Village Other*, ©1968 R. Crumb, originally published by *The East Village Other*.

Page x: "Freak Out Funnies," *Zap* #0, ©1967 R. Crumb, originally published by Apex Novelties.

Page 22: "Lenore Goldberg and Her Girl Commandos," *Motor City* #2, ©1970 R. Crumb, originally published by Rip Off Press.

Page 38: "Eggs Ackley Among the Vulture Demonesses," *Big Ass* #1, ©1969 R. Crumb, originally published by Rip Off Press.

Page 56: "Fritz the Cat Superstar," *The People's Comics*, ©1972 R. Crumb, originally published by Golden Gate.

Page 70: "Ooga Booga," *Zap* #4, ©1969 R. Crumb, originally published by The Print Mint.

Page 83: *There's No Business*, artwork ©1984 R. Crumb, originally published by Black Sparrow Press.

Page 84: "A Gurl," *Big Ass* #2, ©1972 R. Crumb, originally published by Rip Off Press.

Page 85: "Whiteman Meets Bigfoot," *Homegrown Funnies* #1, ©1971 R. Crumb, originally published by Kitchen Sink Press.

Page 86: "That's Life," *Arcade* #3, artwork ©1975 R. Crumb, originally published by The Print Mint.

Insert:

Page 1: *Despair* #1, ©1970 R. Crumb, originally published by Last Gasp Eco-Funnies; *Motor City* #1, ©1969 R. Crumb, originally published by Rip Off Press; *R. Crumb's Head Comix*, ©1968 R. Crumb, originally published by Ballantine Books; *Big Ass* #1, ©1969 R. Crumb, originally published by Rip Off Press; *Uneeda Comix*, ©1970 R. Crumb, originally published by The Print Mint; *Zap* #1, ©1967 R. Crumb, originally published by Apex Novelties; *The East Village Other*, cover artwork ©1970 R. Crumb, originally published by *The East Village Other*.

Page 2: *Heroes of the Blues*, artwork ©1980 R. Crumb, originally published by Yazoo Records.

Page 3: *Early Jazz Greats*, artwork ©1982 R. Crumb, originally published by Yazoo Records.

Page 4: *Bottleneck Guitar*, artwork ©1975 R. Crumb, originally published by Yazoo Records; *Louie Bluie*, artwork ©1985 R. Crumb, originally published by Arhoolie Records; *The Hokum Boys*, artwork ©1975 R. Crumb, originally published by Yazoo Records; *Harmonica Blues*, artwork ©1976 R. Crumb, originally published by Yazoo Records.

Page 5: *Rompin' Stompin' Ragtime*, artwork ©1974 R. Crumb, originally published by Yazoo Records; *Memphis Jug Band*, artwork ©1979 R. Crumb, originally published by Yazoo Records; *R. Crumb and his Cheap Suit Serenaders*, artwork ©1976 R. Crumb, originally published by Blue Goose Records; *Maxwell Street Alley Blues*, artwork ©1974 R. Crumb, originally published by Barrelhouse Records.

Page 6: *Pioneers of Country Music*, artwork ©1985 R. Crumb, originally published by Yazoo Records.

Page 7: *Les As du Musette*, artwork ©1994 R. Crumb, originally published by Oog & Blik.

Page 8: *Carload o' Comics*, ©1976 R. Crumb, originally published by Belier Press; *Mr. Natural* #3, ©1976 R. Crumb, originally published by Kitchen Sink Press; *Weirdo* # 14, ©1985 R. Crumb, originally published by Last Gasp Eco-Funnies; *Raw* Vol. 2 #3, cover artwork ©1991 by R. Crumb, originally published by Penguin Books; *Homegrown Funnies* #1, ©1971 R. Crumb, originally published by Kitchen Sink Press; *Arcade* #6, cover artwork, ©1976 R. Crumb, originally published by The Print Mint; *R. Crumb's Fritz the Cat*, ©1968 R. Crumb, originally published by Ballantine Books.

Page 87: "You Can't Have Them All," *Hup* #4, ©1992 R. Crumb, originally published by Last Gasp Eco-Funnies.

Page 88: "Karen Meets Boz," *Weirdo* #3, ©1981 R. Crumb, originally published by Last Gasp Eco-Funnies.

Page 89: "Psychopathia Sexualis," *Weirdo* #13, ©1985 R. Crumb, originally published by Last Gasp Eco-Funnies.

Page 90: "Big Fine Legs," *Black and White Comics*, ©1973 R. Crumb, originally published by Apex Novelties.

Page 112: "Keep On Truckin'...," *Zap* #1, ©1967 R. Crumb, originally published by Apex Novelties.

Page 134: "Amerika," *Introducing Kafka*, artwork ©1994 R. Crumb, originally published by Icon Books, Ltd.

Page 152: "Jumpin' Jack Flash!," *Thrilling Murder Comics* #1, artwork ©1972 R. Crumb, originally published by The San Francisco Comic Book Company.

Page 168: "Ain't It Nice?," *Arcade* #6, artwork ©1976 R. Crumb, originally published by The Print Mint.

ACKNOWLEDGMENTS

WITH DEEP GRATITUDE, THANK YOU:
Corin See, my editor at St. Martin's Press, for his enthusiasm, support, patience, and guidance.

WITH DEEP APPRECIATION, THANK YOU:
Doug Allen, Chuck Alverson, Bob Armstrong, Joel Beck, Ivan Brunetti, George Carlin, Dan Clowes, Joe Coleman, Dana Crumb, Robert Crumb, Dame Darcy, Kim Deitch, Don Donahue, Roger Ebert, Will Eisner, Jim Fitzgerald, Mary Fleener, Lora Fountain, Drew Friedman, Josh Alan Friedman, Terry Gilliam, Al Goldstein, Justin Green, Bill Griffith, Matt Groening, George Hansen, Steven Heller, Jim Jarmusch, Jaxon, Jay Kinney, Denis Kitchen, Peter Kuper, Mark Landman, Don and Darren Levey, Jay Lynch, Walter Minus, Alan Moore, George Paulus, Charles Plymell, John Pound, Trina Robbins, Eric Sack, Richard Sala, Frank Stack, Spain Rodriguez, Ivan Stang, Ralph Steadman, Robert Storr, John Thompson, Marc Trujillo, Tom Veitch, S. Clay Wilson, Jim Woodring, and Ray Zone.

FOR HER GOOD WILL, PATIENCE, AND UNDERSTANDING, THANK YOU:
Becky Hall.

MONTE BEAUCHAMP

is an art director and designer, and the creator/editor of the Harvey Award-winning *Blab!* magazine. His work has appeared in *Print, Communication Arts, American Illustration,* and the *New York Festivals Annual of Advertising.* He has received numerous advertising awards, including five New York Festival awards for excellence in print and television communications. He lives and works in Chicago.

C O N T E N T S

FOREWORD

Cartoonist: The Simpsons, Life in Hell

When I was a kid I had to hide my R. Crumb comics from my parents. Now I'm a parent, and I have to hide my R. Crumb comics from my kids. Thirty years on, and I'm still hiding my R. Crumb comics.

I've been digging Robert Crumb's work since 1967, when I was a sulking thirteen-year-old Boy Scout in Portland, Oregon, who'd just finished reading *Catch-22* and realized everything in my life was wrong. My pals and I were would-be hippie dorks, only our parents made us mow the lawn and cut our hair, so we made up for our outward wimpiness by goggling at the weirdest hodgepodge of freakish music, art, and writing we could get our hands on—stuff like Frank Zappa's *Freak Out!*, Tuli Kupferberg's *1001 Ways to Beat the Draft*, M.C. Escher posters, the Fugs' *Virgin Fugs*, and various underground newspapers, psychedelic flyers, and "Big Daddy" Roth hot-rod model kits.

Then one sleepy afternoon I was perusing the latest issue of

1

Eye, a glossy ersatz youth-culture magazine, and right there, on the back of the poster that came stapled in every issue, I found myself staring, in a quivering mix of pleasure and disbelief, at a postage–stamp–sized reproduction of the cover of *Zap Comix* #1! I didn't know it till that moment, but it was exactly what I'd been looking for throughout my entire pubescence!

I raced downtown to the Longhair Music Faucet, provider of all my psychedelic-culture needs, and sure enough, they had *Zap* in stock. Oh yeah! There it was! Mr. Natural! The Snoids! Meatball! Thank you, God, even though I'd been doubting Your Existence these last few weeks! And thank you, R. Crumb, for giving me a comic book that was completely familiar yet utterly strange, like some odd, parallel-universe mind-warp cartoon combo-platter of Basil Wolverton barflies, background characters from E.C. Segar's *Popeye,* and grinningly psychotic bear cubs from some sleazy 1950s funny-animal comic!

I was hooked. I was in heaven. I stopped drawing Batman parodies and started my own pathetic version of *Zap,* which I called *Boing Comics.* My chums and I quit the Boy Scouts—we literally ran out of our final Scout meeting screaming our heads off—and we pored over those early issues of *Zap,* looking for secret clues. We tried to figure out how to crosshatch like R. Crumb, but man, did our stuff look lame. I remember how we used to fantasize about the future—the 1980s, we figured—when we'd be able to saunter over to the bookshelf and choose from several hardbound volumes of the collected works of Robert Crumb—and damn if that little dream didn't come true!

Then one day in 1969 I came home carrying *Zap* #3 and #4, which I left on my desk while I headed for the kitchen to make a peanut-butter sandwich. When I returned to my basement bedroom, the comix were gone—but I just figured I must've hidden 'em away. It wasn't until that night, when I heard Dad bellow my name in a particularly bellicose way, that I suddenly realized something had gone disastrously wrong with my *Zaps.* It turned out, I soon learned, that my younger sister Lisa had swiped the comix and showed them to my youngest sister Maggie—and of course their unclean giggles had immediately aroused the suspicion of Mom. So there stood Dad, who normally was pretty tolerant of my trashy taste—after all, Homer made surfing movies and was a cartoonist himself—and he and Mom were livid.

"We never believed in censorship," Mom said. "Till now."

"Judas priest!"—his strongest curse—Dad muttered, shaking his head in disgust.

I slouched in shame. I apologized profusely and swore I'd never bring comix into the house again. From then on, I was really careful about where I hid my comix.

Shame and lying and hiding were my only options at the time, but even then I took comfort in the sheer exuberance of Robert Crumb's work. It took a few years to think it through, and the fact is, I'm still thinking it through, but I remember realizing early on that Crumb was a genius, obviously—and that part of Crumb's genius lay in his unwillingness to hold himself back. Unlike most of the rest of us, Crumb's not trying to be liked for his work, but instead makes a pretty decent offer: here's my life, my art, and my fantasies, on my terms. Crumb's stuff, whether funny or chilling, is proffered in a friendly enough manner, but underlying it all is an offhand, casual invitation: Take It or Leave It, Pal.

"When I take LSD, I see Robert Crumb's world," one of my sophisticated, drug-ingesting high school buddies told me, and having minimal first-hand psychedelic experience, I'll have to take his word for it. For me, beyond the kick in the ass that acid gave to Crumb's work in the sixties, is the experience—rare in cartoons—of stories that deal with the fundamental unsolvable human problems of sex and desire, loneliness and love, aggression and anger, despair and terror—all executed in that freakishly talented Crumb style. The combination of human feeling, great art, snappy writing, and original thought in Crumb's work makes for a powerful wallop. He's unafraid to tackle any

3

subject, uncompromising in his transgressive attitudes, and completely willing to portray himself as a fool. You may not share Crumb's fixations, you may not be as alienated by the nearby shopping mall, you may not be obsessed with Crumb's idea of callipygian beauty, but it sure is a relief to read someone's beautiful Bad Thoughts and realize the world won't come crashing down after all.

I've met Crumb a few times, and each occasion was memorable for me, if not for him. I'll tell just one story: December 1984, in Hollywood, when I hung out with Crumb, Greg Gannon, and Gary Panter for part of an afternoon. As we drove down Hollywood Boulevard, Crumb kept wryly muttering, "It's a cold, cruel world, full of mean, hateful people," while he intently hunched over his sketchbook, drawing constantly. Suddenly he looked up and said, "Pull over! Pull over!" We stopped in front of the Church of Scientology, which had set up an elaborately fake Xmas wonderland diorama in its parking lot. It looked like one of Crumb's *Frosty the Snowman* comics, complete with a phony Santa's workshop covered with plaster snow and plastic icicles. Crumb dashed over to the cardboard–brick donation well, squinched up his face in the best Scrooge-like fashion, and had Gannon snap his picture while he extended his index finger and thumb to drop a penny in. Then we popped back in the car, and Crumb went back sketching and back to his litany: "It's a cold, cruel world, full of mean, hateful people."

In preparing to write this introduction, I went back to my bookshelf and pulled down all those comics, sketchbooks, collected works, interviews, and assorted Crumb-related novelties. I swore I wasn't going to gush, but after looking through all his stuff, ruminating about it for a few months, and sitting here winding this piece up, there's no getting around it:

It's a privilege to gasp and stare and laugh at his work, because Robert Crumb's the best.

T E R R Y   G I L L I A M

Film Director: Fear and Loathing in Las Vegas, Brazil, 12 Monkeys

In 1963 I was working for Harvey Kurtzman as the assistant editor of *Help!* magazine. One day these extraordinary pen-and-ink drawings turned up from some kid in Indianapolis—or somewhere in that direction. They were tales of a sexy cat called Fritz. We published them. Sometime later the guy turned up in New York. His drawings gave no hint of what he looked like. We were surprised.

Bob has always looked the same—long, tall, stooped, and somehow lost—but in those days he didn't have a mustache. But he had the famous thick glasses with which he has always managed to view the world with astounding clarity. And he had his gang of acolytes and big-boned women which always seemed to follow him.

He wandered around New York eternally in awe, but never romanticizing, scratching away in his sketchbooks. We sent him to Harlem. He sketched, he survived, we published the results.

He gave me the impression that he thought of himself as a

kind of nobody, a nothing. The rest of us were the cool, hip, successful ones. Of course, he was totally wrong. He was the one getting laid, he was the one receiving constant adulation, he was the one we all admired, he was the genius—but he managed to avoid recognizing it and being corrupted by it.

He went off to Europe. Harvey paid him to send back sketches. He sketched Bulgaria.

Back in New York we hung out together. He helped populate one of our fumettis along with other friends—struggling writers, cartoonists, and actors, all who fluttered around the guttering flame that was *Help!* And then Harvey closed down the magazine.

Bob became the great underground cartoonist.

I didn't see him for twenty-five years until the night of the 1990 Academy Awards. *The Adventures of Baron Munchausen* had been nominated for four awards and my wife, being one of the nominees, dragged me along to the ceremony. We lost on all fronts, and while the other awards were being doled out, we escaped to the bar. All the losers were there and, as I pushed my way through the tuxedoed crush, there stood Bob … wearing a baggy tux and porkpie hat, looking eternally out of place. Everybody had a drink in their hand. Bob had his sketchbook. He was scratching away for some magazine—just like the last time I had seen him. It was as if nothing had changed in all those years. But things had. He had a mustache.

Writer: Tales of Times Square, Warts and All

My introduction to the work of R. Crumb came about in the East Village, after concerts at the Fillmore. I discovered militant newspapers, *Screw*, and underground comix around the little kiosk headshops of the day, whilst awaiting a ride back to Long Island. Here was the equivalent of an ancient Arabian trading district, with illicit and subversive delights beyond our suburban reach.

My copies of *Zap*, *Bijou Funnies,* and *Yellow Dog* fit on the same shelf with my Fillmore programs and hash pipe. S. Clay Wilson and R. Crumb became my two fave artists. There was a comix rack at the old hippie Bookmasters on Fifty-ninth Street that became my supply line on trips to the city.

Though life in school was horrible, I remember the magical new world of drugs, underground comix, "underground" music, and the spectre of having sex. Crumb's art was able to shock me—and what a nifty adolescent experience! His images are like statues in my memory: the father commanding his wholesome daughter, "Sis," front and center for a blow job; the sweating Snoid, a little nothing of a man who inhabits women's bungholes, overwhelmed by his own erection; Angelfood McSpade, who seemed like Crumb's idea of a good time; and those covers depicting city street landscapes. His characters became folklore. They illustrated subjects I had previously only joked about with select disturbed individuals.

Even after my fifty comix were bagged away, I kept peeling out the one with "Whiteman Meets Bigfoot." This is perhaps the greatest love story I have ever read. I reread it every year for a decade, choking back emotions at the same parts. I remember arguing with somebody's mother twenty-two years ago, who said it had "no literary worth." It is a great comic novel.

I've often fantasized about getting to make a movie out of S. Clay Wilson's characters. But Crumb's "Whiteman Meets Bigfoot" would make an extraordinary film, especially with the technology to build an abominable snowwoman. Alas, it would be impossible to make in a Hollywood system gripped by mental illness and cowardice.

Crumb's new strips are terrific and he refuses to commercialize. The worst anyone can say about his work is how it's "matured." But then he goes and does something like "If I Were a King," steeped in the same old infantile sexual obsessions. God bless him.

D O N   D O N A H U E

Underground Comix Publisher: Zap, Mr. Natural

❚ first met Robert Crumb in 1967, when he was twenty-four and I was twenty-five, in San Francisco, the city of my birth. I was already involved in the underground publishing scene and had been so for a long time, starting when I was a seventeen-year-old beatnik putting out a poetry magazine. In 1967, I was working for *The Berkeley Barb*.

Crumb had arrived earlier that year from Cleveland. There was an underground paper in Philadelphia called *Yarrowstalks* that had printed some of his work. The third issue, in fact, was entirely by him, and was such a success that *Yarrowstalks*'s publisher, Brian Zahn, asked him to do a comic book. Crumb had wanted to draw a comic book before, but this was the first time anyone had offered to publish one. He dashed off two complete comics, *Zap Comix* #1 and #2, and sent issue #1 to Zahn. Then Brian Zahn (who could have been called the father of underground comix) did a surprising thing. He disappeared along with the artwork. Someone in his office said he had gone to India. (Seven years would pass before Crumb's lawyer tracked Zahn down and recovered the artwork.)

I had seen Robert's work in *Yarrowstalks* and in *The East Village Other*. Although there were other underground cartoonists (notably Joel Beck, Gilbert Shelton, and Spain) whose work turned up here and there, Crumb was instantly in a class by himself. His archaic drawing style captured the essence of early-day comic art without being an imitation of any one artist. The content, on the other hand, was definitely post-LSD. The bottom line was genius.

When I met Crumb, he was still wondering what had happened to Zahn and he had an unpublished comic book that was supposed to have been the second issue of *Zap*. Sensing history in the making, I told him I was a publisher and I would print it for him. So *Zap* #2 became *Zap* #1.

I hired printer Charles Plymell to run off the cover and the pages. I couldn't pay him, having zero capital, so I gave him an expensive tape recorder. The books were assembled, folded and stapled by Robert, his wife (Dana), me, and various friends. The four thousand copies sold out quickly through the underground distribution network, although we didn't make much money with a cover price of twenty-five cents.

Plymell decided to move to Canada, so I took over the payments on his press and other equipment, and started learning how to print. My first job was a second printing of *Zap* #1 (five thousand copies) that was paid for in advance by legendary Berkeley bookseller Moe Moscowitz on behalf of his friend Don Schenker, proprietor of the Print Mint. The Print Mint had started out as a framing shop and had become a major distributor of rock posters and underground papers.

By an amazing stroke of luck, Crumb had made Xeroxes of the original *Zap* #1 (the one that was missing) to send to a friend in New York. The friend returned them and Crumb touched them up so I could use them to print from. He decided that the book should be numbered zero to preserve the sequence.

Back when Plymell was printing *Zap* #1, Crumb asked me if I had some company name that I wanted to put on the cover and I thought of Apex Novelties. When he redrew the cover for *Zap* #0, he created the logo of the heart inside the lightbulb.

So I had been a printer for a month and was still learning how to run the press, and I already had more work than I could handle. Meanwhile, three more artists had gotten in on the act: poster artists Victor Moscoso and Rick Griffin, and S. Clay Wilson (who had just come out from Kansas). Together they cranked out a fifty-two-page book, *Zap* #2, that I was supposed to print. This was an overly ambitious task for my little press that printed only two pages at a time. Nevertheless I attempted it, but it was taking too long, the artists were getting impatient, and Don Schenker was waiting in the wings with enough money to pay for a downtown printer who could do the whole job in a couple of days. So the inevitable happened: the artists apologetically informed me that they had to go with Schenker, which caused me to break out in red spots.

Fortunately for me, Crumb was working on yet another project, one that was perfectly suited to my capabilities. This was *Snatch Comics*, the ultimate (at that time) challenge to censorship: a pocket-size comic that was too hot for the Print Mint to handle. So I became, for a while, a publisher of porn. There were *Snatch* #'s 1, 2, and 3, *Jiz*, and Rory Hayes's *Cunt*, all of which were printed and distributed in an atmosphere of secrecy and caution.

Since no commercial bindery would touch them, these books were assembled on a piecework basis by various hippies who would come by with suitcases to pick up the pages and covers and would return with completed comic books, which were then sold to various entrepreneurs who came to my loft. Some of the books ended up under the counter at head shops; some were sold from under people's jackets on the street; and, of course, a great many ended up spread all around the country (and indeed the world) through various underground channels.

Through the first half of the seventies, I maintained my printing business and occasionally put out comix such as *Mr. Natural* (with Gary Arlington), *Your Hytone Comix*, *Funny Aminals*, *Black & White*, and others. Also posters and note cards. But all the real excitement for me was back there in the first two years of underground comix.

Underground Cartoonist: Bijou Funnies

Fascinated by the *Playboy* mystique, I moved to Chicago in 1963. It was a time when Hef was hip, and the goal of all young red-blooded American cartoonists was to appear in *Playboy*. Back then Skip Williamson lived in Canton, Missouri, and Art Spiegelman lived in Rego Park, Long Island. The three of us had been in contact for several years through the humor/satire fanzine network, the spark of which surreptitiously ignited at the beginning of that decade and was destined to explode into the fifty-megaton blast that was the underground press of the late sixties.

The three of us were young beatnik cartoonists. We lived for thrills and kicks—but we were constantly governed by a moral imperative manifested to us in the didacticism of our hip media role models. We were kids with full-formed superegos which were shaped by the discourses of Kurtzman, Krassner, and Lenny Bruce, as well as the old Corlis LaMont brand of Ethical Humanism;

General Semantics; Zen Buddhism; Albert Ellis's Rational Living; cool jazz; and countless other ingredients thrown into the proverbial pot of our belief systems and brought to a boil by our raging adolescent hormones to be served up as our ethical-reality stew of that era. This recipe hasn't changed much since then. A dash or two of fresh First Amendment–freedom condiments may have been added in preceding eras—but essentially, we three kats have always reserved the right to season to our own tastes. In the early sixties, when this was a new recipe to us, we liked the stew's taste so much that that we decided to devote our lives to force-feeding it to the anorexic Society-at-large. The name of this delectable dish? Responsible, didactic satire.

Me, Skip, and Artie—it was in the cards that the three of us would ultimately do a satire magazine together that would call society's bluff. In 1966, Skip cashed in his chips and moved to Chicago. By the summer of 1967 the two of us, amply assisted by Artie via the U.S. mails, were ready to go to press with the first issue of *The Chicago Mirror*. We had intended the thing to be a local satire magazine, incorporating the same iconoclasm as Krassner's *Realist* and the popular British satirical weekly *Private Eye*. All of a sudden, though, even before the rubber cement of the paste-ups of our first issue had dried, the whole hippie thing started to take off. Our perceived audience of local beatnik intellectuals was turning into a zoned-out flock of cosmic-conscious love babies. Loss of ego boundaries among our readers didn't mix with our penchant for editorial cynicism. We toned it down. We tried to speak to our readers in their own lingo, but somehow hippies and satire just didn't seem to mix.

We had known of Robert Crumb's work. We watched it evolve from the late fifties stuff he did in his fanzine *Foo* to the incredible sketchbook features he did on Bulgaria and Harlem in the pages of Harvey Kurtzman's early sixties humor mag *Help!* Harvey had a section in *Help!* called *Help!*'s Public Gallery, which featured the work of Crumb, Shelton, me, Skip, Terry Gilliam, and a long list of other young cartoonists—the talents of whom Kurtzman recognized early on in their careers. Around the time the third issue of *The Mirror* hit the stands, Crumb published *Zap Comix*. I was in touch with Crumb and Shelton (who was then living in Austin, Texas, and doing comic strips in *The Austin Rag*) through the mail. Gilbert wrote me praising the first issue of *Zap* and telling me of his plans to publish his own book, *Feds 'n' Heads*. Skip and I had been doing surrealist comic strips in *The Mirror*—but the bulk of our output in those days was one-panel gag cartoons for men's mags and publications like *The Realist* and *The Idiot* (a satirical mag put out by James Wojack—a San Francisco satirist who ultimately gave up publishing his mag and joined the merchant marine). Excited by Crumb and Shelton's use of the comic strip medium in this new directly accessible format, the underground comic book, Skip and I decided to try it ourselves. It elated us that people would actually accept a thirty-two-page all-comics magazine. Before *Zap*, adult comics were relegated to sections of noncomic publications in the tradition of *Playboy*'s Little Annie Fanny or *Cavalier* magazine's Charlie Charisma strip by Hank Hinton (another *Help!*'s Public Gallery alumnus). We ceased work on the fourth issue of *The Chicago Mirror* and concentrated our efforts on getting together the material for *Bijou Funnies* #1.

Crumb came to Chicago for the Yippie festival at the 1968 Democratic National Convention. He crashed at my pad while he was here and, together with Skip and Jay Kinney, helped put together *Bijou* #1. We got a cheap printer named Lenny to print the thing. I was working at an art studio then, designing medical magazine ads for Lomotil, a diarrhea suppressant. My salary paid for the printing of *Bijou* #1. The title took off. It was hot. Soon I quit my job and devoted all of my time to the comix thing.

Because the restrictions of the Good Comics Code, which applied to newsstand comics in those days, posed a direct challenge to us (just as the old Hays office posed a challenge to the motion picture industry in the three decades following its formation), it was inevitable that both of these genres would rise to the challenge as they did. Both comix and films reached their creative peak as a direct reaction to the challenge of censorship. It all reminds me of a cartoon by Heinrich Kley which has always formed an almost iconological image for me. In the first drawing, Kley depicts a centaur sitting on his haunches and holding a guitar. "And why shouldn't I play the guitar?" it is captioned. The second illustration shows the centaur wildly strumming the instrument. The caption reads: "Sure I play the guitar. Now all the more." Since I first saw it in the late fifties, this cartoon has always been floating on the top of my aforementioned boiling vat of ethical stew. Freedom, as a reaction to repression, and great art and literature as a reaction to artistic and literary censorship, are the facts of life.

Anyway, in 1967 *Zap* was an idea whose time had come. Crumb's genius assumed the form of a totally new form of cartoon imagery. His eclectic use of the pop culture images from the childhood memories of his readers was infused with the now generation's carpe diem vigor. It was a whole new type of thing. It was the imagery of nostalgia existing totally in the now. A contradiction to everything that had come before it, and a hauntingly fascinating contradiction indeed. Crumb concocted a truly weird universe in his comic strips—a universe that sprouted from the collective unconscious of a generation. Sometimes delighting the reader and sometimes reaching into the depths of the reader's most hidden fears, Crumb brought the sensibilities of the poet to the then–almost totally sterile and infantile field of comic strip art, and things haven't been the same since. *Zap* begat the whole movement that was underground comix, and for me, it was a privilege and a gas to have been a part of it all.

Cartoonist: The Spirit

By the end of this century, comics (as in "comic books") will have grown into literary validity after decades of critical disdain. This is due in no small way to a group of cultural dissidents among whom was Robert Crumb: a talented writer/artist who today is one of the internationally acclaimed cartoonists working in comics.

Around 1935, comic books began as an extension of the daily newspaper adventure strip. Dailies were stacked and compiled into complete stories and published in a standard magazine format. By 1940, they were established as widely popular reading for young people. The stories were addressed to teenagers and younger, and they dealt with adventure. They quickly established themselves as the most popular form of juvenile literature.

For the following thirty years, this remained their underlying direction. The artists and writers in the field concentrated on the development of their draftsmanship and the creation of novel superheroes. The publishers devoted themselves to printing technology and the exploitation of their characters. They sought nothing beyond what had already worked for them. They remained committed to comics as simple entertainment.

Then suddenly, toward the end of the sixties in California, a group of counterculture cartoonists that included Bob Crumb began to produce "underground" comics, devoted to social protest. They were uninhibited, raunchy and irreverent. The appearance of these crudely printed products was arresting. It was clear to me, who had so long believed in the literary potential of this medium, that Crumb and the others had broken through. Their work eschewed any preoccupation with form and concentrated on content. They had a message. Because of what they were saying, they were not part of the mainstream. They violated the comics code, so they had to find other ways to reach readers. They effected a change in the distribution system, they attracted adult readers, and demonstrated the literary capacity of the comics medium. Under their influence, comics had reached maturity. Bob Crumb led the charge. His work in particular contained great, mature social observation and satire. He and his group cultivated the ground that enabled people like me to undertake subjects of substance addressed to an adult readership.

S P A I N   R O D R I G U E Z

Underground Cartoonist: Zap

❚ first met Crumb in New York around 1967. I had come to town the previous winter and *The East Village Other* published a comic by me called *Zodiac Mind Warp*. It was originally intended to be a comic book, but the printer said it was technically beyond him, so we put it out as a tabloid.

There was an underground comix scene that had developed there. I met Trina Robbins, who had a dress shop on Fourth Street. Kim Deitch was doing comics with me in *The East Village Other* and Art Spiegelman had shown me his revolutionary concepts of page layout. Art invited me and Kim to visit him at Topps Bubble Gum and after a false start, we finally made it there.

On our first attempt, we accidentally ended up in Queens. I had a nickel and Kim was broke. We both had hoped to mooch car-fare back to Manhattan from Art, but when we ended up in Queens it was then that we first found out that, money-wise, each of us was in bad shape. We then tried to extract some meager change from the good burghers of Queens, who didn't want to give "nahting" to two hippie vagabonds. Some nice girl finally gave us thirty-five cents and we slunk back to Manhattan.

We finally got to Topps and Art showed us some of the Topps's archives, which included some cards done by Crumb. They were well drawn but otherwise unspectacular. They certainly gave little hint of the storm by which Crumb would take the town a few months later.

And sure enough he did. His first things were strips that were printed in a Philadelphia underground paper. I remember one about two guys battling it out. There was some quality about his stuff that made it look like some old-time thing you dimly remembered as a kid. He seemed to have struck some ancient vein that you find on LSD when you think you've found the key to the universe or something, then forget when the drug wears off. Only he didn't forget.

The budding underground cartoon world was in an uproar over Crumb. He was doing things other guys had wanted to do all their lives. Some went through a deep, personal crisis. Some thought about quitting cartooning forever. Others tried to commit suicide.

Although I liked Crumb's stuff a lot, I didn't see him as a personal rival. I don't do funny comics, and in fact, I'm not even certain that I totally approve of funny comics (or humor in general for that matter). Actually, my personal crisis came later when I first saw S. Clay Wilson's portfolio. We were all so sensitive then.

So anyway, when we heard that Crumb was coming to town we were all real curious as to what kind of guy he was. He was definitely the most polished of all of us. Was he an art snob? Was he a regular guy? Was he some kind of intellectual?

On the Lower East Side, there was never a dull moment. So Crumb found himself smack in the middle of all the riots, rip-offs, and intrigues of the day. He turned out to be a pretty good guy after all, and we showed him around town and made sure no one messed with him.

The place where me and Kim lived on Eighth Street and C was a real hellhole. We lived on the sixth floor. The landlord was afraid to come into the building, so we didn't pay any rent. But the place was run by a gang of Puerto Rican teenagers led by a city maintenance man. Kim had this antiquated pistol with a wobbly chamber that enabled him to get up and down the stairs without any hassles.

Once when we were going up the stairs, some dude in vermilion pants deliberately stepped in front of Robert so he had to walk around him. I nonchalantly slammed into the guy and then looked him in the eye. We proceeded unmolested.

A short time later, Robert went back to California and he published the first *Zap*. It looked real good. It had that quality of something you had seen a long time ago but couldn't quite remember when. It was shortly followed by the second issue with work in it by the great S. Clay Wilson; the lords of the poster world, Rick Griffin and Victor Moscoso; and Gilbert Shelton, whom I regard as the first underground cartoonist.

I made a brief appearance in issue #4, along with Robert Williams. With issue #6, I became a permanent fixture.

Crumb generously gave ownership of *Zap* to the artists, so it's jointly owned by all of us. He didn't realize at the time that this would prevent other artists from coming into the comic and, I think, Crumb has some regrets on that score. On the other hand, having the same artists has given *Zap* something of a consistency to its format and, I hope, a quality that it might not otherwise have had. We are planning a new issue, after somehow having survived through the years, and I for one hope to continue doing *Zap* and underground comix in general for a long time to come.

Writer: The Realist, Rolling Stone, The Village Voice, Playboy

One afternoon in the early sixties, R. Crumb visited me at the office of *The Realist* in New York City. He showed me his scrapbook, and it was as though he had turned himself inside out and his unconscious kept spilling out onto those pages. There were different characters, to be sure, but they were all aspects of his own place on the cusp between self-delusion and honesty, between fear and courage, between humility and pride, between reverence and absurdity. He was truly a renaissance weirdo.

A decade later, Ken Kesey and I were coediting *The Last Supplement to the Whole Earth Catalog*. Kesey had been reading a collection of African parables and the moral of one was, "He who shits on the road will find flies upon his return." I asked Crumb to do the cover illustration, totally trusting his talent, and he sent us his version of the Last Supper, with Jesus sharing that ecological haiku with his disciples while a phonograph played "Help Me, Rhonda."

23

More recently, in the final issue of *Weirdo* magazine, he went all the way in revealing nothing less than the slimy tentacles of our national id with the publication of two comic strips, "When the Niggers Take Over America!" and "When the Goddamn Jews Take Over America!" "It's a complicated mixture of feelings and attitudes that are impossible to explain," he explained. Crumb had merely dived headfirst into the abyss of political incorrectness, serving as a one-person antidote to what he refers to as "mass–media–friendly fascism."

After I saw the movie *Crumb*, it was not such a great surprise that he wanted to discard his public identity. For Crumb's cartoons had always been smaller than life, as if seen through a microscope. But now, suddenly, there he—and his marvelously dysfunctional family—could be seen on the big screen, *literally* larger than life. He was no longer just an observer. He had become the observed. Nevertheless, Crumb continues to shine through in a culture where irreverence has become an industry.

J A X O N

Underground Cartoonist: Skull, Slow Death, Comanche Moon

By 1968—with the dance poster scene mostly spent—San Francisco artists were looking for a new energy focus. R. Crumb's *Zap* provided it: black-and-white mind-warp comics, easy to produce and sell, with "anything goes" as the subject matter. The newsprint "guts" were sandwiched between an eye-catching cover, its hand-separated colors often suggesting the same psychedelic matrix that had spawned posters.

Comics like *Zap* weren't altogether new, of course, but there is no denying that this issue really launched the "Underground Comix" trip. It came at just the right time and place to inspire the artists clustered in San Francisco to give the experimental vehicle its thrust. This in turn served as a beacon to induce other artists to move to the West Coast or start their own books in more tuned-in cities around the country. But—as with posters—Frisco was the energy center, and its productions continued to mold the emerging art form.

The comix trip has been fairly well chronicled in two 1974 books. Mark James Estren's *A History of Underground Comics*, a slick, fat offshoot of the *Rolling Stone* publishing empire, is perhaps the better known of the two. It was welcomed by the artists (because of the recognition, i.e., the vanity factor) but was also resented by them (because of the big bucks that Estren and his capitalist-pig-pretending-to-be-hip publisher would make off "our" energy). The other study is called *Artsy Fartsy Funnies* (a terrible title), by Patrick Rosenkranz and Hugo Van Baren. It is a funky seventy-eight-page essay published in Holland—of all places—but jammed with vital information. In a sense, Rosenkranz and Van Baren's book is closer to the spirit of comix than the elaborately produced (but now falling apart, due to size and shitty glue) Estren book. Rather than attempt to rehash what these capable "authorities" have done—especially in acknowledging the catalytic role of Crumb's *Zap*—let me simply outline how I wandered into this madness.

The reader should always remember that the comix work being discussed *speaks for itself*. Thus, other than providing a little background, historians (even the artists themselves) can't help a lot by commenting on the whys and wherefores of various creations. Often such jabber only distracts from the personal meaning that these books had for each of us during our first encounter with them. It might even lessen or destroy their impact, by layering over with crud the flash that they elicited from our minds so long ago. Kind of like watching the movie *Giant*, now that we know Rock Hudson had AIDS; it just ain't th' same anymore....

This is the risk we run in dissecting such things, whether in the spirit of rational inquiry, homage rendering, or just plain muckraking. Since we humans are incapable of "leaving it alone," whatever "it" may be, the topic of comix cannot expect to escape similar scrutiny. I want to express my genuine suspicion of all such analytical exercises before adding more crud. Happily, nothing I've ever read about Joe Kubert has ever dimmed the flash that his comic, *Tor*, beamed at my juvenile brain back in that 1950s Texas drugstore, so I trust that it is possible to intellectualize about comics and still retain the primal bliss.

Before getting sidetracked on this ramble about the futility of criticism/adulation (after all, what's done is done; why bother with it?), I was going to try and remember exactly how my brain cells became so befuddled, or, to be precise, how I got mixed up in a crazy business like drawing and producing comic books instead of working in a bank, selling insurance or practicing mortuary science. But it's not easy—at this stage of terminal mind rot—to recall all the waves that gently slapped against my small boat, driving it ever so imperceptibly toward the swirling maelstrom.

As a child I was taught that things were predestined; that one's fate was written before the earth was created, somewhere beyond the stars; and that our only purpose here is to act out what was foreordained. A chilling prospect for those who set great store on individual accomplishments, but rather comforting for those who dread making decisions (or taking responsibility for them). So when I found myself scribbling and doodling away on Big Chief tablets as a kid, I figured it was meant to be. Though incapable of articulating it, I knew that some cosmic force was acting through me, not to be deterred. Contentedly, I kept filling those pads with little drawings and, in time, became pretty good.

It was a way to get attention, quite honestly, some of it encouraging, some not. I soon noticed that "neat" people liked my drawings, whereas "clods" didn't. I did not copy other drawings at first (that came later when I saw the comic book *Blackhawk*); I just drew cowboys and Indians, GIs and Japs, or the usual dumb-shit stuff. By the time I was in high school, I discovered *Mad* magazine, acquired its "sick" perspective, and learned that girls were impressed by my budding skills. Since I had no other skills to speak of, my course was set (R. Crumb, does this sound familiar?). Whether predestination had been involved I still don't know, but to this day I feel that artists shouldn't take a whole lot of credit for their accomplishments. If something of value flows *through* them, they should count their blessings rather than toot their horn. Alas, we live in a world where blessings don't count for much unless one toots one's horn. Perhaps that's why artists tend to see themselves as their own worst enemy and are so fucked up in general. Beneath all the pretense, they know they're cashing in on a gift.

Going to Austin in 1962 from my rinky-dink little college in South Texas—where I had quickly lost interest in being a CPA—I got my first taste of art for art's sake. It came in the form of the University of Texas humor magazine, *The Texas Ranger*, paid for by the Journalism Department to give students a working knowledge of how to turn out a "professional" product. The irony was that only a fraction of the people involved were journalism students. Since nobody seemed to mind, we used the *Ranger* as a vehicle to publish zany stuff, as daring as we dared.

After each month's issue, the lunatic fringe who had attached themselves to the mag would throw a rip-roaring party, liquor compliments of UT. With a deal like that, no wonder so many fun-loving folks became professional students and lingered around campus for years. The *Ranger* was a self-perpetuating party scene, always the center of action and populated by the brightest people in a six hundred–mile radius. It was there that I met artists like Gilbert Shelton and others who would later figure in the doings on the West Coast. As I look back on it, the comix scene that emerged in San Francisco wasn't really all that different from our miniversion in Austintacious: a bigger stage, more players, but the Texas contingent had already learned the basics of putting out humor magazines, thanks to the *Ranger*.

One thing we hadn't learned about was the grueling economics of the business, for the mighty UT system had always picked up the tab. Reality hit when the entire staff was sacked for a violation of someone's nebulous editorial guidelines. Our offense: we ran a photo of a braless hot tomato, her full, firm breasts ever so discreetly peeking through a sheer blouse—yum, yum. After this rude awakening to the power of purse-strings censorship, a few of us (Shelton, Tony Bell, Joe E. Brown Jr., and myself) rallied off campus and put out a hopelessly pathetic imprint called *The Austin Iconoclastic Newsletter* (*The*, for short). We even issued several magazines under this title, but it didn't last long. *The*, however, taught us how tough it was to indulge your fantasies when the production money had to be self-generated and when the artists/writers had to do everything from selling ads to handling pasteups to hustling the result on the streets. These lessons came in handy when members of our disgruntled clique later started Rip Off Press.

Sometime during this do-it-yourself period, my *God Nose Adult Comix* came out and was sold to the UT student crowd in similar fashion. It was really nothing but an elaboration of the concept found in *The* and in Frank Stack's *Adventures of Jesus* comic, which had been printed in Xerox form and circulated around Austin for a while. *God Nose* is truly an "underground" comic, though, for it was printed in the *basement* of the state capitol, just before I quit my straight taxman job (as had been foreordained, of course). The proceeds from the thousand-copy edition of *Nose* sent me on a scenic tour of Europe by motorcycle in the dead of winter. With me was one of the *Ranger* crazies and later cofounders of Rip Off Press, J. David Moriaty.

After freezing my butt off abroad, I returned penniless to the States via New York. There I met R. Crumb through some resident Texans and got turned on to his work. As I recall, he was doing something about black folks in the slums for a Kurtzman mag; I was impressed. By this time, the old scene in Austin was somewhat dispersed, accounting for Joe E. Brown's presence in the Big Apple. Many Austinites had formerly looked to the East Coast as a cultural fount/party scene, but the Village was on its last legs, creatively speaking, and the coffeehouse circuit was already becoming commercialized. Word of exciting new happenings on the West Coast began to trickle back to Austin, and Venice/Frisco soon became the destination of most Texan "freaks." The redneck mentality, by 1966, was growing oppressive. When drunken "cedar-chopper" rowdies began to frequent the bars around campus—long a safe district for social deviants—I knew it was time to seek a more tolerant climate.

I hit San Francisco in mid-'66 and found the Promised Land. Although the beatnik scene on North Beach was still chugging along, "hippies" were beginning to congregate in the Haight, and the ballrooms and dance halls were where the real action was. I learned that Chet Helms, a long-haired poet from Austin's party days, was throwing weekly dances at the Avalon Ballroom on Sutter and Van Ness. His outfit, a loose conglomerate of artists, musicians, dopers, and "beautiful people" called the Family Dog, was on the cutting edge of something big—what, no one knew, for the media hadn't yet caught onto the trip and told us. After six months of straight drudgery in the financial district, I cut loose to work for the Dog. My life since has never been the same, for which I am eternally grateful to the Great Scriptwriter in the Sky.

During my tenure at Family Dog "running" the poster operation, I met most of the craftsmen who created the genre of psychedelic art. I also learned about the four-color printing biz, as well as having to develop a national distribution network for our posters (mostly head shops). These contacts were simply carried over when the poster market became glutted with crap and the artistic community shifted its attention to comix.

As with the beatnik–hippie evolution, the poster–comix shift was a gradual thing: one did not cease before the other commenced. Artists were still doing dance-poster and music-oriented gigs when comix started to be produced. It was a smooth transition because many of the poster artists were also into comics. Some, like Griffin, Moscoso, and Irons, had already used cartoon motifs in their posters. In addition to these "established" artists, others with a preference for the comic strip medium had begun to migrate to San Francisco. Various ones tried, without success, to break into posters or album covers, as that was the paying market at the time. But—by 1968—much of the initial glow of the poster trip had waned; repetition was setting in, and the stores were crowded with mediocre stuff. The time was right for something "new." We didn't exactly like it, but we all realized it: Peter Max had made psychedelic art a cliché and had, almost overnight, stripped the medium of its soul.

Strolling down Haight Street one day in 1968, I was pleasantly surprised to see R. Crumb out there hawking a comic book. It was an honorable method of spreading the word (and eliminating the middleman's cut), one that I had used with *God Nose* in the fall of 1964. Imagine my joy at running into Crumb again and realizing that someone was still interested in comics, even though his Mr. Natural was a direct steal of my God Nose character (just kidding, Robert). Without a doubt, *Zap* #1 rekindled in me (and others) the desire to join in. The San Francisco dope culture had always tended to take itself a little too seriously for my liking. In Crumb's work, I sensed a breath of fresh air—just what we needed if the scene was to remain vigorous and not become smothered by its own self-righteous pomposity.

Zap was soon attracting considerable interest among the disenchanted poster artists. With Crumb's Haight Street debut, other cartoonists started coming out of the woodwork. It wasn't long until the merchandising system—already in place because of the now-fading demand for posters—moved to accommodate their work. The Print Mint in Berkeley, one of the leading poster distributors, began a newsprint anthology called *Yellow Dog* and started pushing individual books like *Zap* as well. Shelton, who had continued doing comics in Austin, was ready to make the West Coast migration. After one of my periodic visits back home, we drove out in his beat-up Plymouth with boxes of low-budget *Feds 'n' Heads* in the trunk. Soon the Print Mint was handling it and a reprint of my old classic, *God Nose*, along with a few other titles.

In 1969 Shelton and I, with several other expatriate Texans—Fred Todd and Dave Moriaty—chipped in and bought a Davidson printing press. We dubbed it "The Rip Off Press," a name more than justified by our lack of printing expertise. Still, we managed to land some counterculture jobs. Among them were posters for Soundproof Productions—the "Texas Mafia" successor to Chet's Family Dog scene at the Avalon. Almost from the beginning, comix were also being cranked out, only natural considering our history and the fact that we shared space in the old Opera House with Don Donahue (Apex Novelties), Crumb's publisher. Most of the books printed before the place burned down were handed over to the Print Mint for distribution, as we had no easy way to push them ourselves and stayed too stoned to bother. At the time, Print Mint's cash-up-front policy for delivered books looked awful good.

Such enthrallment didn't go far. Convinced that the artist's (and printer's) cut was way too small, we expanded the concept of ROP beyond mere production. Between Shelton, Crumb, myself, and other artists like Irons, Sheridan, Schrier, Wilson, Deitch, and "Foolbert Sturgeon" (creator of the seminal *Adventures of Jesus*), we soon had a competitive organization going. The Print Mint's *Zap*, however, remained the premiere showcase of the movement. Nothing could touch it, in sales or in attracting new talent. After S. Clay Wilson's outrageous stuff made its way into the pages of *Zap*, all the underground artists (even Crumb) were hard pressed to produce wilder sexual fantasies. Sex, of course, sells, and in those days, being busted for it was a mark of distinction. How times have changed....

Fortunately, several of *Zap*'s artists also gave work to Rip Off Press, especially the popular Crumb and Shelton. With Shelton's *Freak Brothers*, ROP began to rival the print runs of Crumb's brainchild over in the East Bay. It was a friendly rivalry, though, because the trip was gaining momentum and so much of the energy was shared. If Don Schenker was miffed because certain artists were growing greedy and unwilling to trust blindly his stewardship at Print Mint, it didn't show. The same applied to Donahue's Apex Novelties and Ron Turner's Last Gasp, another outfit that launched itself in 1970 with an ecology-oriented comic, *Slow Death*. We were one big happy family. We partied together and worked together, and there were no bad vibes because of "business," a problem that had plagued the Fillmore and Avalon operations from start to finish.

Apart from the comix that appeared in *The East Village Other*, most of the New York–based talent drifted into Frisco. Thus the creative scene was further strengthened, and the Bay Area publishers had an ever-increasing talent pool on which to draw. There was enough work being produced to keep all the publishers busy. Strong echoes reached us from Chicago (with *Bijou Funnies*); from Milwaukee (with *Mom's Homemade Comics*); and from Los Angeles, where the artists either sent strips to San Francisco (like Robert Williams) or put together their own titles. Austin managed to carry on without us, as a new crop of artists had arrived and based themselves at the Vulcan Gas Company and later Armadillo World Headquarters—Texas's answer to the California dance emporiums.

Amazingly, many people in these cross-country enclaves already knew each other, or at least their work, dating back to such showcases as Harvey Kurtzman's *Help!*, hot rod/surfer 'zines, or even the college humor magazine era. As suggested by the reference to *EVO*, underground newspapers were often an early route to strips being gathered in book form. Ron Cobb's cartoons in *The L.A. Free Press*, Shelton's strips in *The Austin Rag*, and stuff printed in Madison's *Bugle-American*, Philadelphia's *Yarrowstalks*, and Berkeley's *Barb*—to name a few—laid the groundwork for later anthologies. More than one cartoonist seeking work with West Coast publishers displayed his or her underground newspaper strips as "credentials" in the comix vein. We could all relate to such experience; most of us had paid dues in similar fashion, before comix provided an alternative.

It's been thirty years now since *Zap* #1 hit the street. Comix, if regarded as a vestige of the counterculture, has certainly outlasted most other art forms spawned by the sixties craziness. Though not as exciting, perhaps, as it was in the Glory Daze (what is?), the phenomenon continues in a number of titles. R. Crumb is still at the forefront. He remains a dominant force, and sure as hell has kept more of his old fire than his counterpart in the music world, Bob Dylan. Perhaps the poverty of graphic artists, relative to rock stars, does have its redeeming value. At least it keeps them hustling to survive, i.e., doing creative work instead of coasting for years on fat residuals until they have nothing interesting left to say.

Could comix have happened without *Zap*? Probably, but why bother with "what ifs"? The fact is, *Zap* kicked it off in grand style and gave the movement a kind of energy that hasn't yet spent itself. When future historians of the comic book medium look back at the results, Crumb's genius will shine through and the offerings of the "mainstream" industry will pale beside it. You can take that to the bank, folks.

R O B E R T   A R M S T R O N G

Musician: The Cheap Suit Serenaders

With all the hoopla surrounding Terry Zwigoff's fine documentary, *Crumb*, enough has been said in the press about Robert Crumb's dysfunctional upbringing, his particular sexual obsessions, and his comics, which are often interpreted as sexist and/or racist. So I won't bother you with my views on those subjects. But there is one aspect of Crumb's life that was barely touched upon in the film, and that is his deep affinity to certain styles of music.

As long as I've known the guy I've found that music, especially the type found on old recordings from about 1926 to 1932, is every bit as important to his life as drawing and sex. The lure of money and fame is not a motivating force for Crumb. He can remain coolly detached from opportunities and financial gain that most other artists only pray for, but dangle a rare 78-rpm record in front of him and he'll practically be on his knees. He loves old records with a passion. But in all fairness, his love of music transcends merely owning the recorded disc. He can be deeply moved by a musical performance and the social conditions that contributed to it. He's confessed to getting teary-eyed while listening to records whether they be by blues singers, hillbilly string bands, novelty groups, jazz bands, popular dance orchestras of the day, or any manner of ethnic music recorded by immigrants in the U.S., or by performers captured on disc in Europe or elsewhere. In fact, as record collectors go, Crumb is fairly unique in his wide range of interests. While most collectors have specialized fields of interest, Crumb has sought out the best of all musical genres of the period. As long as the music is heartfelt, dynamically performed, not slick in a commercial or overly professional sense, and is genuinely interesting, he'll listen intently.

But Crumb isn't just a passive listener. He's been inspired by the old platters to play music himself on banjo, guitar, mandolin, and accordion. Far from being a virtuoso on any one instrument, his approach is loose and sort of funky. But Crumb possesses the unique ability to capture the feel of a particular style. Not one to simply ape a studied performance, copying it note for note, he instead gets to the essence of the sound and comes up with his own interpretation. Crumb also has a keen memory for melodies and has a good sense of harmony. When Al Dodge, Terry Zwigoff, and I would work up material with Crumb for the Cheap Suit Serenaders, it was Crumb's ability to work out the chord structure of a tune that we learned to depend on.

Another thing about Crumb's musical sensibilities that I've always appreciated is his willingness to explore musical forms that others would find contemptibly corny. When I first met him about twenty-five years ago, I was pleased to find that he shared my love for old Hawaiian and polka records—two particular styles that at the time were unanimously shunned by all other collectors. It's not that he found the material delightfully silly or campy; instead he recognized each for its overlooked inherent beauty. Crumb's appreciation for musical forms abandoned by the general listening public goes hand in hand with his preference for music performed by the nonprofessional. Recordings from sixty to seventy years ago included a lot of rich music made by regular working people who entertained themselves at home or performed in their immediate region. This, of course, was before radio and television got a stranglehold on public tastes and virtually killed off most of the personal and regional styles that made up the patchwork of American vernacular music.

Along with Crumb, I've always preferred music that is accessible and lacks pretense. This reminds me of a particular instance when he and I were in Aspen, Colorado, in 1972, wandering the streets one evening looking for something to do. The ski resort scene, filled with bronzed bimbos and the full array of insipid ski bums, was making us both feel uncomfortable. While walking past a closed bakery, we heard some group singing from an open second-story window. We invited ourselves in and found that the singing was coming from a large group of teenage girls with just a couple of very nerdy guys present. It must have been some church group, since everybody looked so wholesome and well scrubbed. (We never did find out what it was all about.) They were all singing really corny old favorites like "I've Been Working on the Railroad," "Polly Wolly Doodle," etc. Crumb and I made ourselves at home and enthusiastically joined in. After a while we were leading the whole group, suggesting old standards that everyone could sing a few choruses of. The girls seemed to think we were really great, much to the chagrin of the teen guys present. After the girls provided us with a couple of guitars, we were the center of the whole sing-along party. I've never seen Crumb so happy. And if those girls only knew what kind of comics he liked to draw....

T R I N A   R O B B I N S

Underground Cartoonist: Wimmen's Comix, Wet Satin

In the winter of 1968, I had a boutique in New York's "East Village" (really just the Lower East Side) and was trading clothes to the editor and staff of *The East Village Other* (*EVO*) in return for them running free ads by me for my boutique in their paper. The ads were really comic strips and were so low-key that most people didn't even know that they were ads. So in a way, I was sponsoring my own comic strip.

Underground comix were really in the Stone Age during this time. Back then, they existed in the form of one-page strips that appeared in the underground newspapers of the day. I knew Spain and was somewhat familiar with his work, and I had seen earlier strips in *EVO*—one called *Captain High*. But the one which, when I saw it in 1966, inspired me to draw underground comic strips was called *Gentles Tripout* by Panzika, who I later found out was a woman, Nancy Kalish. I'd also seen the work of R. Crumb in

Yarrowstalks and even earlier in, I think, *Help!* magazine, and I thought that it was brilliant. In those days his work was very sweet and what stood out about it was his nostalgic-looking style. However, it still hadn't occurred to me that underground comix could appear anywhere else but in underground newspapers. I mean, like, the only comic books back then were just Marvels and DCs.

I'd already learned from my experiences the previous winter that February is a dead month for boutiques—nobody's buying—so I sublet my apartment and went back to California for the month. I'd been living in Los Angeles before I moved to New York and I returned there to visit friends. While I was there, I took a side trip to San Francisco and was met at the airport by some friends who were aware that I was into underground comic strips and knew that I would react as I did when they did what they did, which was to hand me a copy of *Zap* #1 without saying a single word. And I reacted as they knew I would—it utterly blew my mind! For the first time, I realized the possibilities. One didn't have to be restricted to drawing strips for underground newspapers; you could actually do an entire *comic book*! I can't begin to describe what a revelation this was to me; probably a lot like what discovering Jesus is to "born-again" Christians. In a way, knowing that I could do a comic book was very much like being "born again."

For about a week, I stayed with my friends in a Victorian flat across the street from Golden Gate Park and I searched for Crumb on Haight Street. At one point, I just missed him. He and his wife had been walking up and down the street peddling copies of *Zap*. About half a year later, he came to New York and I finally got to meet him. This was about the time he was making the transition from his nostalgic/psychedelic style to the violent misogyny that characterized his work throughout the rest of the sixties and most of the seventies.

I remember the first one of those newly styled misogynist strips of his that I saw. Crumb had just drawn it and I eagerly started reading it, expecting it to be another one of his typically sweet comics. But by the time I got to the end, I was horrified! It was very hostile to women. Now, I hadn't even heard of the term "women's liberation" yet—I don't think the term had yet been coined—but I knew antiwoman hostility when I saw it. And this strip, along with those of Crumb's that followed, contained a lot of it. The thing that was so frustrating to me was that none of the male cartoonists would acknowledge this hostile element in Crumb's work (even though Crumb himself readily admitted it, and I can think of at least three instances in his comics where he admits it on the printed page). And my insistence about his hostility to women simply got me into a lot of trouble with the then–underground comix establishment. To these guys, Crumb was sacrosanct, and criticizing him was a sin that earned me ostracism.

I remember an interview with Crumb, written by a guy I knew, that appeared in *EVO* in which Crumb mentions that I accuse him of hostility to women in his work. The interviewer defends Crumb by saying, "Sure you're hostile, but you're just putting yourself in the role of a little boy and all little boys are hostile to women." And Crumb replies, "No, I'm not pretending to be a little boy. I'm just me—twenty-six years old—and I am hostile to women!"

It's weird to me how willing people are to overlook the hideous darkness in Crumb's work. I mean, the other underground cartoonists (all, of course, male) used to tell me it was all just satire and that I had no sense of humor. But what the hell is funny about rape and murder? (Of course, men are *always* saying that women have no sense of humor!) But then, ironically enough, when I did draw the very few comics that I did which showed hostility towards *men* in them (and I did them in answer to the great outpouring of antiwoman hostility in the undergrounds of the early seventies), the *men* wildly overreacted with comments such as "Hide the knives" and so forth.

I guess the worst of it to me is that Crumb became such a culture hero that his comics told everybody *else* that it was okay to draw this heavily misogynistic stuff. The phenomenon of the underground comix of the seventies, so full of hatred toward women, rape, degradation, murder, and torture, I really believe can be attributed to Crumb having made this kind of work stylish.

And then, weirdest of all, is *People* magazine coming out with an article on Crumb in 1985 about how cute his Keep On Truckin', Fritz the Cat, Mr. Natural, and maybe a naughty naked tit are. But it's like, these people haven't *really* looked at Crumb's work because there's no awareness of the really *hideous* things he drew: of Jumpin' Jack Flash fucking a mound of dead hippie chicks; of Angelfood McSpade being screwed while her head is submerged in a toilet bowl; of the chicken woman's head being cut off by the Cute Little Bearzy Wearzies; of Forky O'Donnell stabbing his girlfriend to death with a fork and showing the body to his friend, who in turn says, "Let's fuck it!"

Ironically, just as R. Crumb was responsible for the birth of the underground comic book, I believe he was responsible for its death. Because he *was* such a culture hero, his comics became the major inspiration for eager new would-be underground cartoonists who adopted his style, complete with the rampant misogyny, often doing him one better. Soon the stands were loaded down with underground comix that featured graphic rape scenes and every other degradation toward women that the writers/artists could think of. Entrails, usually female, were scattered over the landscape in a phenomenon of violence to women that I believe has never been equalled in any other medium. Unfortunately (or perhaps fortunately) these wanna-bes lacked Crumb's talent, so the stands were loaded down with *badly drawn* misogyny. The work of some of these people, such as Rory Hayes, was so bad that it was a novelty for a while, but there really is just so much of that stuff that people can take and the comic-reading public soon reached its limit.

I certainly grant Crumb a tip of the hat for getting the underground comix movement started. I'm just sorry that he took a wrong turn in Albuquerque.

THE REVEREND IVAN STANG

Writer: The Book of the SubGenius, High Weirdness by Mail

Robert Crumb is one of my heroes, and heroes are important—they can make you want to stay alive when you aren't sure whether you've been left behind, or are about to be run over, by the Trend Monster. They keep you running ahead of it or, better, running off down roads it can't navigate.

I have to explain this Trend Monster first. It's not really a solitary monster but is composed of a few thousand people and their styles. There's an extremely fast turnover rate, though, so nobody is part of it for very long. You can visualize it as a huge wad of flesh, bristling with people and beliefs, barreling down a curving highway—actually *building* the highway as it goes along—or as a kind of fleshy meteor careening randomly through outer space, sucking in the nothingness in front of it as it moves, but crapping out a trail of dollar bills, ideas, and people into the void behind it—all rendered useless because they are no longer *in* the Trend. It only needed them for exhaust; they are the fuel that power it along, and when they're burned up, they're left behind as empty, shucked husks. It's a little like a high-speed chain gang, except that you don't have to commit a crime to be sentenced to it—even nice people get dragged in. (Most live, physically, in L.A. or New York City while they're astrally imbedded in the Monster.)

The Trend Monster is constantly changing shape, of course. It's in perpetual metamorphosis, because there's always new fuel. Most of this fuel is provided by people who have been running at top speed to catch up with it and join it. They don't know the danger—that they'll just become fuel—because they cannot recognize the burnt-smelling litter it has left behind as having once been fellow people.

There are other people standing here and there in the path of it, and they get scooped in, too.

There are always far, far fewer people actually composing the Trend Monster at any given time than there are being left behind. The moving Monster is always outdistancing the vast majority, who trot somewhat lazily behind it, only halfheartedly keeping up the appearance of trying to "catch up"—most of them perfectly satisfied to have grabbed their own piece of it during the brief time it was passing them, or feeding off them.

But there are even fewer people, only a few hundred at any given time, who manage to continue running *ahead* of the Trend Monster. Robert Crumb is one of these. He's frantically scurrying along, trying to stay ahead of it, occasionally getting tired out and almost getting caught in it. Indeed, he *was* caught in it once—that's the stretch of highway way back there that's so bumpy and strange-looking.

It's really hard to be in this position, because you aren't actually *on* the highway (you're ahead of what's being built) and you have no idea what direction the Monster is going to take. You have to run while constantly glancing backwards at the Trend Monster, trying to second-guess where it'll veer, because if you make a wrong move, it'll either run over you or engulf you—either way, you'll be ground up and left behind, with everybody else—only it's worse for you because *you'll know what happened.* You now know what the Trend Monster is. But most people don't find that out until they've been through it and been excreted by it, after which it's too late. They've become its garbage, part of the horrible litter on the roadside.

On that patch of road that Crumb was forced to help build, some of us saw the spot where he'd scrawled the truth about the Trend Monster in the fresh cement. These secret instructions made it clear that we, like him, must continue running just ahead of it. Some might even have to overtake it from behind and scramble madly over the top of it, catching a ride for a while in order to pass it, taking care not to actually get sucked in and blown out its behind as exhaust.

It's thankless work, dashing up there in front of it, but at least you know where you stand. You can look back at it and know exactly what it is.

And you can toss nails out behind you as you run.

The nails won't stop it—in case of blowout, it always has some up-and-coming ad exec or politician or actor or rock star to use as a spare—but they'll slow it down until someone figures out what to do next.

Just after I read the letter inviting me to help idolize Crumb—which no doubt embarrasses him—who should show up at my door but Jay Condom, another of my many cartoonist friends and coauthor, with Gary Panter, of *Pee Dog Comics*. We discussed "what Crumb means to us," and it turned out that we'd both had identical experiences when we were teenagers, trying to figure out if we were going to be *hippies* or not. We'd stumbled upon *Head Comix* in bookstores—normal mall bookstores. We'd already heard Jimi Hendrix; we'd seen *Easy Rider* and *Woodstock*. We loved monster movies, but *we didn't know about underground comix*. We were hicks in Texas. As much as Crumb used to bitch about not wanting to be "commercial," if we (and many, many others) hadn't seen that *one commercial book, Head Comix,* we'd never have known that there even *was* such a thing as "not being commercial." We might never have dared enter head shops, which in those days were being watched by police. All the other generic hippie stuff was fun, but we'd *very, very possibly* have been blinded to the dangers EXCEPT FOR THOSE COMICS, and we'd have been blind to the comics—for a critical time, anyway—without Crumb's work being so unquestionably provocative that a large publisher gave it wide distribution.

In all fairness, I should also mention that Frank Zappa served pretty much that same function at the same time. So did the Firesign Theater. They too were running ahead of the Trend Monster. Thank god there were people who, firstly, let us know that the hippies could be as full of shit as their enemies in the establishment, and, secondly, who showed us just how *fun* it could be to *tell the truth through lies.* I don't recall any films or books having had this effect on me. I'm a filmmaker and writer by trade, and influences include everything from Bugs Bunny to Fellini to Kesey and so on, but let's face it, comics have more PICTURES than books, and rock 'n' roll is more important than films, to a teenager. And it's teenagers who are most in need of that kind of deconditioning.

It may have been a life-or-death thing. Speaking personally, I might well have fallen prey to any of those combinations of things that could kill you in the late sixties and early seventies had I not had such vivid examples of what I basically wanted to do, such proofs of what was possible. I had a really shitty teenagehood and a rough early adulthood, psychologically; those defiant voices, Crumb's being one of the most insistent and entertaining, were sometimes the only things worth living for. The acts of defiance, the remembrances of incredibly funny panels and lines and stories, provided meaning in the midst of crappy jobs and bad news and troubled relationships and the ever-present lure of drugs. Kids need meaning even more badly nowadays and I hope my own work can help a little in providing some. Crumb's existence was a hint that you could create something worthwhile without selling out and still get

46

commercial distribution. It's a thin line, but I see no sense in trying for less. If the work isn't in normal stores at least for a while, it'll probably never reach the audience that needs it most. It's preaching to the saved. But if it's too slick, it'll lose its effectiveness just as badly. I know that Crumb, in his more naive days, eschewed copyrights and job offers from the likes of *Playboy* out of idealism, but I hope that he appreciates the fact that his alone were the "underground" comics that leaked out into the "overground" and thus lured us to those secret places where his compadres worked.

And think how he feels, having seen his style copped a million times by everyone from amateur comic artists to big time TV commercial producers, to stinking, blubbering, hideous Ralph Bakshi.

Where did it lead for me? Hell, I'm actually making a living as an underground cartoonist! I just happen to be the only underground cartoonist who can't draw worth a shit, and never drew cartoons. My handicaps forced me to work with film and words instead—but it's basically still underground comix that I do. Very similar pay, very similar *version* of the old underground comix audience. The Church of the SubGenius might as well be a gigantic underground comic book, gone electronic, using video and radio and books—and the brains of the audience—as the canvas. I'd like to take it as far as it can go, into movies and TV if possible, as long as it can retain the integrity—integrity learned from Crumb and those cohorts he pointed us toward. Failure would mean either, on the one hand, losing control and integrity to the Trend Monster, and on the other, never being widespread enough to reach the right audience as thoroughly as necessary.

Crumb's comics also showed us what art really is, at a time when what people called "art" were bloodless abstract designs hanging on museum walls. That legendary vision of the young, nerdly R. Crumb standing on a street corner in San Francisco, hawking *Zap* #1 at twenty-five cents each to anybody who'd walk by, has clung to my brain like a persistent leech, a perfect and pristine picture of the artist *doing what he must do no matter how stupid it looks at first.*

While Jay Condom and I were discussing all this, Jay mentioned the "Whiteman" story, which was reprinted in that old *Head Comix* book. I had almost forgotten the damn story, it's been so long ... but I realized with a shock that he was right—that story, perhaps more powerfully than any other, illustrates the exact manner in which Crumb's work diverged from all before it. He dared to speak what, in those years, was THE UNSPEAKABLE—Whiteman's *fear* of black people, battling inside him with his innate 1960s sense that they were as human as he, or more so—was something that so self-evidently needed to be said that we readers were stunned into a sense of just how painful, and how necessary, telling the truth might be. Crumb's depictions of blacks and women, his big-legs obsession notwithstanding, were understood by us (fellow white male artists) for what they were—far beyond racism and sexism, and in fact, violent reactions against both, using irony and horror as stylistic tools. The vehement responses from shallow feminist trendies and dumb-ass "liberal" do-gooders—outrage and idiotic accusations—also taught us a lesson: that oftentimes, the artist must be ready for the "truth" to be totally misunderstood by the very people in whose behalf it was done.

Crumb's honesty also showed us his own faults—taught us the all-important lesson that our heroes are as human as we. I remember being very disappointed in *The People's Comics*—it seemed evident to me that the many pundits calling him a "genius" had not exactly gone to his head, but had at least caused an ornery reaction—perhaps conscious—which he'd prove otherwise, by hook or by crook. But even in his most pretentious period, which didn't last very long, he was *still* being honest. He let his internal worries over his own integrity *glare through*. He was/is the "Jimmy Swaggart" of comics, but unlike Swaggart, Crumb deliberately let his faults and deepest artistic insecurities out of the bag so that we'd know he wasn't something to put up

48

on an altar and worship. He kept us informed regarding the changes he was going through, in case we might have to go through them. He was always fair with us, much fairer than he had to be.

I appreciate the hell out of it.

(And what did he do in his "down" period? He made goddamn *records*! He went out and, most likely at some personal cost, recorded and released those quirky cover versions of ancient jazzy songs that he and his pals performed—twenty-five years before every high school student with a synthesizer and a dubbing deck was sending out "independent cassettes!" How ornery can you GET??)

Crumb never forgot his own origins as a gawky fan boy for a second. *Weirdo* wasn't just his vehicle, it was also a vehicle for any artist who was struggling and, to him, deserving of first-time magazine publication. A personal for-instance: *Weirdo* #1 reprinted SubGenius materials in 1981(!!), and that single bit of exposure brought us to the attention of half the people who are now mainstays of the whole project. He has been very generous with his time and influence.

He *shared*.

I didn't expect him to like SubGenius when I first sent him a pamphlet; I certainly didn't expect him to write back. To my surprise and joy, he not only wrote back, and plugged us, and gave us free advertising, but he also warned me personally of the psychological traps that await any artist with even modest success. He predicted a whole series of stages I'd be put through in the gauntlet of Art: initial, undeserved overglorification; a period of critical backlash resulting from all the poseurs hating you because you're now "famous," and no longer "underground"; an identity crisis over whether you really HAD "sold out"; and, hopefully, a time of getting back to doing whatever the fuck you wanted to do, audience or not.

Beyond his control, but still of immeasurable value, are the lessons taught by adaptations of his work to other media. The movie of *Fritz the Cat* is the ultimate warning to all artists to never relinquish control of one's character to Hollywood, because once the vampires get hold of it, they'll suck your creation dry and leave it void of any originality it once had. I made a 16mm film of Crumb's junkie tale "Ducks Yas Yas" (*Zap* #0) when I was in high school, whereupon I learned that the best approach is to do your own thing, not "interpret" someone else's stuff. (I chose "Ducks Yas Yas" because it was the only Crumb story I thought might be done right with actors instead of animation [and with no budget], seeing as how I couldn't draw, but was nevertheless inexplicably *compelled* to try making a film of a Crumb piece. Crumb himself didn't like the film much, and I sure don't blame him.)

On a tangent: I also had the good luck to see the only (to my knowledge) stage production based on the collected works of Crumb. The Hip Pocket Theater in Fort Worth ran a play which had an actor playing Crumb (perfectly), narrating and griping his way through interspersed sequences from his comics. When the play had actors playing Mr. Natural, Honeybunch Kominsky, et cetera, it was cute, but it flopped. The stories didn't work except as Crumb comics, *drawn* in his style. On the other hand, the "Crumb talking" sequences worked, and to a T. These were all directly transcribed from the innumerable strips Crumb had done over the years, in which he drew himself, ranting on various subjects. The actor had Crumb's mannerisms down, and the rants were a joy to behold. The final lesson: if you're going to adapt a Crumb piece to another medium, use the Crumb pieces that *aren't fantasy*.

I know the actor had Crumb's mannerisms down well, because I'd finally gotten to meet my hero, two or three times (at a SubGenius show and at comic book conventions). I couldn't believe how accurately he'd depicted himself in his strips. I mean, he was even drooling over fat-butted, big-legged "gurls," right there in front of me, in *real life*. Griping and bitching cynically, just like that "Crumb" character in the strips! The son of a bitch WAS INDEED as honest as I'd HOPED he was! He really did look and talk like the neurotic, compulsive Crumb of his own comic strips. To see oneself as others see us—what a curse that must be.

The most astounding thing I learned about Crumb, during personal meetings, was how ignorant he was of his own audience. He was at a comics convention in Dallas; we sat together at dinner. He kind of whispered to me, "All these nerdy little guys with glasses!! Are these people the ones who've been buying my stuff all these years??" He was actually surprised. I said, "Well, yeah, of course! Haven't you ever been to a comic book convention?" "No," he replied. I was floored. This was in goddamn 1984, for god's sake!! He was appalled to discover the nerdy quality of his fans. "It's really depressing. They're such geeks!" I did a kind of double take. "Look who's talking, Crumb! *You're* a nerdy looking guy with glasses; I am, too! Most of 'em *are* nerdy geeks, but you can't second-guess what these people are *really* like, any better than they can guess what you or I are really like!" That was a weird experience. I can offer no theory to explain this particular hole in Crumb's knowledge. I mention it only for history's sake. Surely he must've known that most of his readers were Foonts, not Naturals! Yet, I swear, he really seemed to expect his fans to be *normal* or something. It was very strange.

Despite that mystery, I still identify with Crumb. (Of course; I'd even resemble him physically if I were taller and skinnier, and had such bad posture.) Eccentric as he is, he's got enough "everyman" in him that just about anybody can identify with something in his comics. That's what makes his work so … so … I dunno what; it's like he's intuitively managed to cut through a lot of bullshit and go *straight to the point*, a hard proposition in this overly complicated society. You can't quite put your finger on the whys and wherefores, but the guy has tapped some very basic archetypes of the collective unconscious and all that other Jungian stuff. Moreover, they were *previously untapped* ones. Now, THAT is an accomplishment.

51

I promise you that, had there never been a Mr. Natural, then Philo Drummond and I never would have recognized the SubGenius head mascot, "Bob" Dobbs for what he is.

The other day I walked into a local bookstore, looking for children's books. Imagine my glee at finding my own second book, *High Weirdness by Mail* (an encyclopedia of weird publications of *every* kind), prominently displayed right next to the reprint of *Head Comix*. Both from the same publisher (Simon and Schuster) and editor (Tim McGinnis), and both selling well. Ahhhh, yes. Sweet vengeance on the normals. Hope for the teen mutants. A few bucks in royalties for me and Crumb.

It was a great honor. And it has been a great pleasure (and an overdue debt a bit more paid off) to contribute to this salute to Robert Crumb. Thanks to modern communications, he gets to read it while he's still alive—for better or worse.

J I M   W O O D R I N G

Cartoonist: The Whole Earth Catalog, Frank, Heavy Metal, Jim

I have an image in my mind of the unborn shade of R. Crumb, naked and defenseless on a desolate plain, scurrying evasively as God chases him to catch and stuff him full of talent and brains. The terrified, keening ectoplasmorph dashes this way and that to escape, but to no avail; God captures him and Crumb is visited by the Funnel.

This metaphor seems apt to me because I've always felt that there was something weird about the extent of Crumb's ability. Why should he have so much more power than anyone else? What does this portent-that-walks-like-a-man signify?

When I was a teenager and the first *Zaps* were coming out, me and my cartooning pals would gnash our teeth in envy over his work. As a cartoonist he had every virtue we desired for ourselves: his style was fully developed, original, familiar, relaxed, versatile and brilliant, and it was unreservedly praised by art-conscious adults. He himself was, by all accounts, self-deprecating and down-to-earth, an appealing and hip misfit who turned down *Playboy*'s slavering advances on grounds of artistic integrity (that *really* got me). My pals and I knew that if we were going to make our marks as cartoonists we had a long hard road ahead of us, whereas Crumb was obviously a natural whose drawing ability was innate and whose path seemed not only straight but greased.

And was he aware? Did he truly see? *Eeyow*! During the late sixties it was as if the cosmos had dispatched him to the scene of our crime to record and reflect it for us. At that time, you may recall, tribalism had been introduced into our nontribal culture and there had arisen a hybrid—the Hippie. Crumb was poised to capture and distill their brief flowering and the beginning of their multigenerational decline. In those days, the unbelievably apt images in his comics glowed like charged filaments. We laughed hysterically, we stoned ones, laughed helplessly in wonder at the fantastic consciousness on display in his work.

And who else has delivered on a promise like Crumb has? Who else has lived up to a great name made early like Crumb, making his dray-horse way through life, drawing, drawing, building greater mansions by the decade, producing work of which every page is a testament to the relentless striving of a genius?

You can see that to me Crumb was a larger-than-life figure. For years it was my greatest desire to meet him, or at least see him in person, see the actual structure that housed his mighty spirit. When I lived in San Francisco, I went to every gathering and every event that I thought he might show up at. I saw the Cheap Suit Serenaders perform numerous times, but never with Crumb in the lineup. I sent him a few letters, expecting and receiving no replies. I began to wonder what I would be willing to put up with in order to meet him. I wondered, for example, if I would be willing to meet him on the condition that he be drunk and piss on my leg. If the offer had been made in those days, I really would have had to think about it.

One day in 1984 (yes, 1984) my wife and I attended the Los Angeles premiere of Terry Zwigoff's early Crumb documentary, a short video. We didn't expect Crumb to be there, but he was. My shaky attempts at conversation met with humiliating deflection by my hero, but he took a real shine to my wife. He was nuts about her, laughing and friendly and charming: but every time he looked my way, he sneered. Not a slight sneer but a broad, ugly, vaudevillian grimace of contempt that could have been read from a passing airplane. My wife was thrilled; I wept on the ride home.

But that's neither here nor there. Crumb is the greatest cartoonist there ever was and the greatest there ever will be, and I feel privileged to share the planet with him.

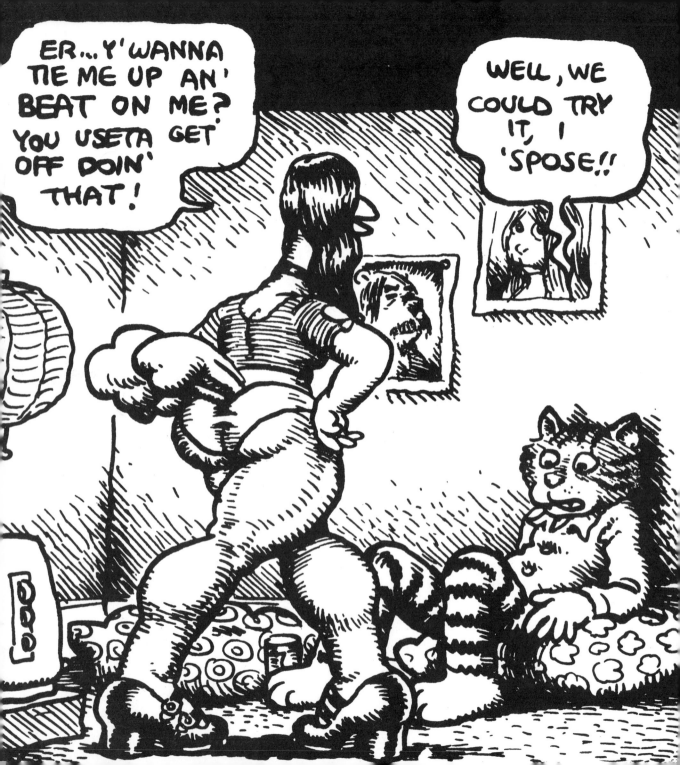

A L   G O L D S T E I N

Publisher: Screw Magazine

Most of the soldiers in the war for sexual freedom are, in a personal sense, damaged goods. From Margaret Sanger to Larry Flynt, the people who have moved us forward on the path toward liberation have themselves been personally twisted in some essential way. Among them—probably one of the most crippled of the bunch—is R. Crumb.

Crumb reminds me of the antiwar book, *Johnny Got His Gun*, the hero of which was a quadriplegic, just a stump of a man, nothing more than a mind attached to a failing body. Crumb's consciousness has been bent by life to an amazing degree, yet the result is not disability but genius.

Crumb is filled with more neuroses than all the patients crowded in the waiting room of some high-priced Fifth Avenue analyst. He's a walking mental institution. In the movie *Crumb* you realize how close genius and self-destruction really are, how

"Fritz the Cat Superstar" The People's Comics, ©1972 R. Crumb; detail

57

madness and brilliance meet, touch, bond. Art is what brings back genius from the edge. In the film, we saw Crumb's brother suffer anxiety and madness unmitigated by the kind of coherent vision Crumb employs in his brilliant comics. The demons pounded on both Crumb brothers, but only Robert was able to fight back successfully with his pen.

I recall visiting Crumb in 1988, in his home outside San Francisco, before he and his family moved to France. I met a man who I thought was even more twisted than his artwork. Alongside of Crumb, and even with all my myriad fixations, anxieties, and neuroses, I felt healthy.

"I don't think America respects people who devote themselves to something like sitting alone doing artwork rather than being out there hustling," Crumb told me in my interview with him.

Crumb's taste in women runs to large-boned grotesqueries with big calves and thighs and massive power. He himself is rather frail, and the resulting image is of "the flea fucking the elephant." When I suggested this to him during our interview, Crumb accused me of "putting it rather unromantically."

But that image fits R. Crumb well—the frail, psychologically misshapen artist-flea, fucking the elephant of American culture. In this case it's clear that the "fucker" is getting off way more than the "fuckee"—but that's always the way it is. Here's hoping R. Crumb has many more humps left in him.

JOHN THOMPSON

Underground Cartoonist: The Berkeley Barb, Eternal Comics

After graduating from the University of California, I lived in Berkeley and worked at my job as a conscientious objector in Oakland's black ghetto. During this time I also worked as a political cartoonist for *The Berkeley Barb*.

On Sunday evening, March 31, 1968, LBJ appeared on my television looking just like the grotesque caricatures I'd been drawing of him for the *Barb*. My wife Gwen and I were startled and pleased to hear him announce he wouldn't seek another term. This caused some optimistic feelings in Berkeley's radical community, but the glow didn't last long. Just a few days later, I was helping a black activist church group put their monthly newspaper together when the radio blared out a special news bulletin: Dr. Martin Luther King had been shot outside his motel room in Memphis.

Countless other civil rights and antiwar activists like myself were stunned by the news. This began the bleakest four months of my life. For the past three years my friends and I had been idealistically committed to struggling with the crucial social issues of the day. Our optimism peaked during 1967's "Summer of Love," when Gwen and I lived both in Berkeley and in San Francisco's Haight-Ashbury. The further we got from that idyllic summer, the more violent things seemed.

It was during this darkest period of my life that I met Robert Crumb. I had marveled at the first cartoons he offered through the Underground Press Syndicate and I reprinted them in the *Barb*. In April, I visited New York and drew some covers and cartoons for *The East Village Other*, a paper that had just printed some of Crumb's drawings. They told me he had moved to San Francisco, gave me his address, and suggested I give him a call.

Back in Berkeley, I phoned Crumb and introduced myself. He was familiar with my poster and cartoon work, so he sounded intrigued when I told him that Joel Beck and I were trying to convince Don Schenker of the Print Mint to publish an underground newspaper of just cartoons called *Yellow Dog*. Bob said that he didn't drive but that he was planning to be over in Berkeley that week, so I gave him directions to the Clifton Street store where Gwen and I lived.

Hearing his knock at the door, I opened it up and was startled to see someone who definitely did not look like the flower child I imagined him to be. My first impression was with how unique he both sounded and appeared. He looked not at all like my hippie artist friends, but in his own way he was even more striking. Although he was a year or two older than me (age twenty-two), he looked even younger, had a gangly thin frame, short hair, and thick Coke bottle glasses.

He scrutinized a copy of an esoteric cyclopean comic that I had drawn, published a few months earlier in an edition of a thousand copies. He also looked over some of the comics my friend Joel Beck had published. Then he briefed me on a project that he was trying to launch: his own comic book—*Zap*.

Crumb's *Zap* bore the influence of Basil Wolverton, an obscure 1940s cartoonist whose work I admired for its funkiness, yet his storytelling skills had the flow of Carl Barks, who drew the Donald Duck family comics for Disney. I showed Bob my own comic book collection of old, yellowing, ten-cent comics and he found some that intrigued him, telling me that he too collected comics.

The next week, I visited Bob in the old wooden Victorian flat that he was renting just a couple blocks south of Haight Street. I met his extremely glum and quite overweight wife, Dana. Dana had dark stringy hair and looked miserable—very out of place in the exotic Haight. Bob told me that he was born in Philadelphia, the son of a low-income marine and a rather heavy mother. He and his brother loved reading and drawing comics when they were young. When he graduated from high school in 1962, he went to work for the American Greeting Card Company in Cleveland, working all day in a little cubicle. He met Dana, and the two of them created a special and personal world out of their young love. They were married.

Bob told me that just a few months after they were married, he rode home as usual on the bus. But instead of getting off at his usual stop, he got off at the end of the line and walked west, and kept walking and hitchhiking with no destination in mind, ending up in Haight-Ashbury. He phoned Dana a couple of weeks later and she was frantic. He explained that he'd left his life in Cleveland behind him. But Dana, who was pregnant, came out to the West Coast to join him. This, Bob explained, was why Dana looked so miserable.

Crumb told me that he had been taking his work around to various publishers and although they seemed to sincerely like his work, there had been no buyers. He'd met with Chet Helms of the Family Dog and submitted designs for posters. Chet said, "These are great, but it's not the sort of image we're trying to convey." I showed *Barb* publisher, Max Scheer, more of Bob's work, but he said it didn't have the sort of social or political views he wanted.

I introduced Joel Beck to Bob and they studied each other's work with careful appreciation. Don Schenker of the Print Mint took a strong interest in

Bob's work and liked his submissions to *Yellow Dog*. When its first thin issue left the printers, Bob and I took them up to Telegraph Avenue and sold them on the street corners. Bob very eagerly stopped passersby on the street and told them about the new paper, and lots of people bought them from us.

When a friend of Crumb's printed *Zap* #1, Bob was quite pleased. He and I again stopped people on the street and sold it, leaving stacks of them at various stores on Telegraph Avenue and on Haight Street. One afternoon, we rode the trolley car to North Beach and left a stack at Lawrence Ferlinghetti's City Lights Bookstore on Columbus near Broadway.

We then wandered around North Beach, once a beatnik mecca just across Broadway from Chinatown. Talking animatedly, we discussed ideas for posters and comics. Bob not only had a buoyant enthusiasm, he had a real vision. It wasn't easy for him to find much to relate with in my cyclops comic, but we found a lot more other interests to share. He hadn't participated in the protest movement as I had, but he had been experimenting with what were then called "consciousness-expanding drugs," which worried Dana. She told me that on his "trips," Bob sometimes felt that he was an incarnation of a 1930s cartoonist and, on some occasions, that he was a 1930s cartoon reborn as a human.

Dana sincerely liked my wife Gwen, as there were a lot of qualities in her that were easy to admire. One afternoon, I went over to talk to Bob as he drew in his little studio in the back of their flat. After parking my Norton motorcycle, I walked up the wooden stairs to his front door and rapped three times. Dana answered and greeted me, then introduced me to a pair of nineteen-year-old girls in the front living room. I was immediately attracted to Robin Marmo, a curvaceous blonde whom Bob had befriended on Haight Street.

During the next couple of weeks I saw Robin often, as she and her girl-friend from Watsonville were "crashing" on Bob's living room floor at night. Robin's father had been an Italian-American soldier. He met her mom after he returned from the war, but when he got her pregnant she declined to marry him. The rejection stung him and he committed suicide. When Robin was born into that unhappy situation, her mother didn't really bond with her, so she was given to a grandmother to raise.

Bob liked Robin. Although he didn't enjoy reading poetry, he claimed to appreciate her poems very much. Dana did not appreciate the attention that I, as a married man, was paying to Miss Marmo. What Dana didn't know, however, was that Gwen liked Robin and that my relationship with her was the least of our problems.

Bob's own libido was, as all erotic drives are, simple and direct, yet paradoxically the most complicated phenomenon imaginable. Walking down Haight Street with him, I watched his eyes widen at the diversity of feminine beauty, while I only occasionally did a double take at a gorgeous flower child.

Bob was absolutely awestruck by forty times more women than caught my eye, and listening to any one of them would intoxicate his appetite. Yet it wasn't just the visual and fragrantly olfactory aspects of their images that enthralled him, as he sincerely was curious and amazed as they revealed litanies of issues that they were struggling with: psychologically, socially, and spiritually. The more a feminine acquaintance admitted her moments of confusion and mixed feelings, especially concerning philosophical issues, the more his jaw dropped in awe, appreciation, and compassion.

Thus feminine strength allured his psyche. On one occasion, we both noticed a student who radiated strength, intelligence, and all these other qualities. Bob walked up to this total stranger beaming unself-conscious affection, hugged her and kissed her tenderly. Her initial look of surprise and delight faded quickly to astonished disbelief when it registered that she did not know this man at all.

In discussing women, Bob never made a lurid remark or recalled any sex act. He mostly just described specific women and accurately, at great length, paraphrased their revelations. His unjudgmental style allowed his subjects to speak for themselves without misrepresenting them by critical analysis.

Quite different from his personal life, his artistic life more freely expressed not only his personal neuroses, but the collective dysfunctions of American men, yet with a satirical flair. In his most personal relationship, with Dana and their new baby, he tried to be responsible but hadn't a clue on how to deal successfully with Dana's disappointments and her lowest moods.

A notorious Hell's Angel named Free Wheelin' Frank had come into some royalty payments from a paperback book that Michael McClure had ghostwritten. Inspired by his own psychedelic revelations, Frank had hand-lettered and illustrated his own poetry and had paid for its publication and the rental of a hall in which to recite it. As it was a free event, Bob and I attended and thanked wild-eyed Frank for free copies.

In socializing before and after the reading, Bob scrutinized the outlaw bikers as if he were at a Fellini cast party. The expressions on the faces of the black-leather-jacket men were not quite as intriguing as what Bob saw in the eyes of their women. Biker chicks with fake eyelashes and midrange IQs never even looked at Bob; however, those chicks with subgenius scores and troubled childhoods were drawn to him intuitively. Thus, although he sometimes made geekish cartoons of himself with his thick glasses and protruding Adam's apple, in social settings bright women curiously enjoyed his conversations.

Singer Janis Joplin, who sometime hung out with renegade bikers, found Bob as amazing as he found her. While her considerable wit and talent, and her quieter gentle side, didn't erotically turn me on, there was an electricity between her and Bob. While he designed an album cover for her, I pulled up a stool and watched him as he meticulously inked her outline—in such a way that the caricature glowed with his fondness for her. He also acknowledged that drawing a band member as a cyclops was an idea borrowed from my art, and he freely pointed out a dozen other minor influences.

As for his dealings with equally exceptional men, he said how much he liked my friend Rick Griffin's posters and album covers, so I took Bob over to the basement on Potrero Hill where Rick and Ida were raising their baby, Flavin. Rick and Ida immediately clicked with Bob, and the ensuing two hours of conversation were more lively than any TV talk show today. Bob's observations flowed like a delicious spigot of excruciating details—involving myriads of subjects. A week later at Bob's studio, he showed me a Grateful Dead poster Rick had given him: a pristine uncut sheet from a Honolulu concert that was canceled (today worth seven thousand dollars uncut). Without my even asking, Bob scissored one of Rick's postcard images off the sheet: just one example of how generous he was.

That same month Bob and I noticed a portfolio of pen-and-ink drawings in a bookstore on Telegraph Avenue. Privately printed, they were the work of a young artist who had left Kansas for the Haight: S. Clay Wilson. Although Bob liked Wilson's style, I found it crude and ugly. Wilson seemed to have a visual preoccupation with sadomasochistic pirates, outlaw biker lesbians, crippled freaks, and cruel demons. My first impression of him was that he was likable (and had my "Flower Child" poster on his wall) but had a very magnified view of his own talent. He got along well with Bob, though.

At this time, my female artist friends often discussed the way in which women were being portrayed in art. I was extremely sympathetic with their views: that avant-garde art should portray them in a positive way. The work of Wilson, Rory Hayes, and other underground cartoonists certainly did not meet with my standards of feminine beauty. I tried to portray women as beautifully as I could, such as in my Avalon poster for the Youngbloods performance. When Crumb later began to depict sex and violence in his work in ways that were degrading to women, I made my feelings quite clear: such work was counterproductive to what young idealistic artists were trying to achieve.

My work also appeared regularly in the *San Francisco Express Times*. Barbara Garson, a feminist, had made some money from her play *McBird*, a satire on LBJ; along with her curly-haired radical husband, she founded the paper. I wrote them a review of a later issue of *Zap* in which I criticized the way that women were beginning to be depicted in "hippie" art. Although Marvin vetoed the review, the art editor, Wes Wilson, was very sympathetic to it. Like me, Wes tried to portray feminine beauty in his posters. He didn't like to see sex and violence depicted so grotesquely in the underground press.

One afternoon in July 1968, Bob and I said good-bye to Dana, hopped on my motorcycle, and drove down to Market Street to see a movie. The theater was so crowded at the special "hippie matinee" that I didn't think that we'd get in to see Stanley Kubrick's spectacular new epic, *2001*. When we did get in, we could only sit in the very first row and gawk up at the huge stage and screen. Crumb had taken some LSD, but thank gawd, I declined. Most of the audience seemed to have smoked or ingested something, thinking that it might enhance their appreciation of this science fiction masterpiece.

Crumb stared at the screen wide-eyed and unblinking and seemed to enjoy every frame of the movie. He was so engrossed that at times his mouth hung open and his Adam's apple twitched. The more the special effects and the performances drew me in, the more I empathized with the tension in the script. The final apocalyptic scenes were so personal that I felt the film had been made just to blow my mind and I had an intense anxiety attack: a compulsive urge to run from the theater, my eyes wide open with panic.

Afterwards, Crumb and I discussed the film at length, mulling over the implications and possibilities of man's future that it pointed toward. We found out later that Rick and Ida Griffin were there in the same audience, stoned on LSD.

Later that month Robin and I took Bob to a performance by the Blue Cheer at the Avalon Ballroom. Bob didn't like loud, blaring "acid rock," and this group, whose name originated from a brand of especially potent LSD, turned their amps up as loud as they could. The group featured long-haired

Leigh Stevens on lead guitar. I knew the bassist: short, wiry Dickie Peterson, who now yelled out the lyrics to "Summertime Blues" with vibrant conviction. Drummer Paul Whaley pounded his rhythms so vehemently that his hands bled from the impact, and a couple of times his bloodstained sticks shot out of his hands. The roar of their cacophony at times sounded almost like punk music, drenched in psychedelic angst. The concert was being filmed by a group that was making a proposal for a weekly television program called *Live from the Avalon*. The video cameraman photographed Bob dancing, although I'm sure they weren't aware of who he was, and also photographed Robin and me dancing in the strobe light to "Doctor Please." This was one of the rare times I had seen (what were later called) "rock videos" being made in San Francisco.

Still later that month the doctor told me that he thought Robin and I might have an especially damaging form of VD that soldiers had brought back from Vietnam; one that wasn't responding well to the usual penicillin. So he injected us with a high dose of streptomycin and told us to drive directly home and go to sleep. I dragged my weary feet down the grimy steps of the clinic and out onto the bleak streets of San Francisco.

I walked right onto a movie set where Woody Allen was shooting a robbery scene for his upcoming comedy *Take the Money and Run*. But for me there was no money, no place to run, and no humor in the pain in my crotch. As we drove by the Panhandle in Golden Gate Park, I felt so sick that I had to stop the car and lie down on the summer grass. Robin held my head in her lap as I sobbed convulsively at what a miserable place the entire world seemed.

Ill health, poverty, and unemployment had their influence on my spirits. Gwen filed for divorce on July 22 and the uncontested case was granted on August 8. Her parents paid for her lawyer and I didn't even show up for the hearing, knowing that would speed up the process. I talked to my own parents about the divorce, and although they were sympathetic and very concerned about the trouble in Berkeley, my relations with them were at an all-time low.

They were putting a lot of pressure on me to cut my hair, leave the Bay Area, and conform to mainstream society—something I didn't want to do.

The great stress I was under created an almost constant pain—a pain I attributed to my anger at society. Although I had a very negative view of what I saw in the mirror, women perceived my melancholic suffering as heroically attractive, or at least Robin did. The stress from insomnia, messy living conditions, an irregular diet, watching a friend shoot heroin in my bathroom and so much more was taking its toll. I began to have fantasies of shooting myself or plunging a knife into my intestines, but my thanatophobia made me yearn to survive—acting out some desperate cry for help.

Robin was very nurturing and comforting and she wrote me many lovely poems, but she couldn't lift my spirits.

Depression is a horrible disease that strikes thousands of people in their early twenties each year. Professionally untreated, my disease was a personal agony that just sucked me in deeper. For lots of creative young people, 1967 offered "the Summer of Love" in the Haight; 1968 offered "the Summer of Turmoil" in the Haight and in Berkeley. Like so many others at that time, I wasn't just suffering severe "male mood cycles," I was suffering a myriad of symptoms of profound depression.

The year 1968 was one of great turmoil. Instead of being consumed by it, Crumb transmuted his own conflicts into his early *Zaps*. It's important to remember that only the first *Zap* was a product of 1967's "Summer of Love" and all that buoyant optimism. Crumb's later work was a product of the troubled and disappointing year that followed—and he spoke to the issues of those times in often very grotesque and disturbing ways. Late 1968 and early 1969 were difficult times for Crumb and the other underground cartoonists, and those difficulties had a profound effect on their work.

When Bob and Dana divorced, I visited him in a ratty run-down hotel, and he looked gray and haunted, speaking very little. His angst seemed to dwarf my own suffering and nothing at the time seemed able to diminish it.

A year later he introduced me to Terry Zwigoff, who seemed morosely self-obsessed that morning. I could only wonder why Bob was spending time with someone who on first impression seemed a talentless loser. His camaraderie with Terry seemed unexplainable. A quarter century later, Terry's film about Crumb would reach an audience vaster than anyone ever expected. Bob's brightness shined from every scene in the well-edited documentary, with no hint of the darkest side I had glimpsed when I first met Terry. Yet even within Bob's gloomiest and most nightmarish days, he never abused himself, his talent, or anyone else.

Thirty years later, I certainly don't look back nostalgically on 1968 as the "good old days" in the wild and crazy Haight-Ashbury. Instead, I remember them as very hard times, yet times in which the underground cartoonists were very productive and had a lot to say that was relevant.

A L A N   M O O R E

Writer: Watchmen, From Hell, Swamp Thing

❚ was born in 1953, so the mid-sixties found me at around the dangerous age of fifteen; the age where you've started to become interested in girls, have started to realize that they aren't interested in you, and have started writing morbid poetry about the atom bomb as a result. What differentiated the adolescents of this period from the countless generations that had gone before, however, was that for the first time in recorded history the world itself seemed to have fallen into step with our personal glandular upheavals. The civilization that we saw documented in the newspapers and on TV seemed to feel every bit as hysterical, horny, excitable, and confused as we did. It was all very bewildering and new.

For my part, exposed to the E.C. line of comics and other exotic influences during my formative years, developing a rational attitude to life was the hardest part. After absorbing the razor-edged satires of Kurtzman's *Mad*, I couldn't see the world without also seeing its absurdity. Familiarity with E.C.'s shock/horror line, although it came later, also meant that I couldn't view the situations around me without seeing their implicit awfulness.

On top of all this ambiguity, something new seemed to be happening. Bearing in mind that I was at an impressionable stage in my development, when even the existence of lava lamps seemed to augur a new millennium, I still don't think this sense of cultural metamorphosis was entirely misplaced. The music on the radio was starting to sound very strange, tinged with the uniquely English "Haunted Nursery" psychedelia of the time, and some of the people that I saw on the street were dressing very oddly, wearing fragments of brightly colored old grenadier's uniforms or with Union Jacks hand-painted over their sunglasses so that they couldn't see. I thought it looked great, and beyond the music and the clothes and the colors, I received a very strong impression that there was definitely something out there, something that was going to rip through society and change it all forever.

Even the comics that had sustained me since infancy didn't seem immune from this seismic shock wave. My recent discovery of comic book fandom had led to my discovery of the late Wally Wood's *Witzend*, a publication which, while it might more rightly be considered "ground level," was my first tentative introduction to the concept that along with all this "underground" music I'd been hearing so much about, there might also exist such a thing as underground *comics*. Tickled by Vaughn Bodé's contributions to *Witzend*, impressed by the excellent George Metzger work in Bill Spicer's *Graphic Story Magazine*, I was still, however, totally unprepared for my first exposure to the hard core of the comic book underground when it came a few months later.

I remember the Saturday in question vividly. Morosely wandering around Northampton's town-center market square for want of anything better to do, I made my way to the news, magazine, and comics stand that I had been frequenting sporadically since buying my first Superman and Batman comics there some seven or eight years before. The stand looked the same as ever, with its dull and rounded iron paperweights pinning down the fluttering pages of four-color newsprint and its long wooden boxes of used paperbacks. One novel element caught my eye, however: hanging from the canvas roof of the stand between the unrelenting jaws of a rusted bulldog clip was a magazine that I had never seen before. Its name, spelled out in two bright, primary-colored letters, was *Oz*, and it was England's foremost underground magazine. What seized my attention in that initial encounter was the magazine's cover illustration. There she was in gaudy full-strength printers' ink on cheap, rough, ass-wipe paper. Against a background of palms she stood with one hand raised to her head seductively, pink tongue rolling around her rubbery lips as she gazed out from beneath lowered purple eyelids that matched the areola of her impossibly solid-looking chocolate breasts. In a curiously dated lettering style that somehow matched the tone of the drawing, the legend above her head said "It's Finger-lickin' Good!"

I was in love with Angelfood McSpade.

The shock, the damage wrought upon my nervous system by that one image was complex and, at the time, incomprehensible. With hindsight, however, I think I've come to understand a little of the disorientation induced by my first exposure to the work of Robert Crumb.

Firstly, and most obviously in the case of this particular image, there was the open sexuality. Not having led a terribly sheltered life, I was familiar with the images of sex to be found in the neighborhood magazine racks ranging from *Playboy* through the Fry-the-Krauts-on-Passion-Bridge "Men's Sweat" periodicals of the day, to the soft-core titillation of homegrown products like *Parade*. Judging from the drawings and photographs that graced these magazine's covers, sex was something that was deadly serious, not to say faintly miserable, smothered as it was in commercial gloss and the self-conscious poutings of the ex-stenographers staked out across the center spread.

Angelfood was different. She was wearing, in addition to her grass skirt, a big pleased-with-herself smile rather than the slightly concussed "just raped" look that her cover girl contemporaries were starting to adopt. It was my first taste of the sexual openness of the psychedelic movement, and though it bears little relevance to my overall impression of Crumb's work, it requires mention in these terms just for the personal impact that it had upon me. This is not to say that its effect in other areas was not equally as marked. Sexuality aside, this drawing was subversive.

For one thing, it was subversive in the way it commented upon race. Many cartoonists since Crumb have referred back, ironically, to the stereotyped image of black people that dominated the cartoons of the past. But this was the first time I'd seen a cartoon depiction of the Negro so exaggerated that it called attention to the racialism inherent in all such depictions.

For another thing, the image was subversive in a much more intrinsic way than in the racial commentary of its content. The style was so familiar as to evince a sensation of déjà vu: this was the rubbery American cartoon style of the forties and fifties that I associated with *Terrytoons* and other such notable ventures in the field of animation. As a style, it looked familiar, as if it had always been there, the epitome of all that was conventional and safe in contemporary cartooning … except, of course, that for a cartoon character to display such obvious carnality was unthinkable. Like lysergic acid disguised as junior aspirin, the package was reassuringly innocuous, but the content was liable to affect one rather strangely. This to me was the essence of Crumb's early work—this balancing act between a sense of line that would have charmed the most hard-nosed redneck, and ideas capable of startling the most extreme radical. It's an approach that has made instant twentieth-century archetypes out of even Crumb's most outré creations and, more importantly, has rendered even his most personal visions immediately accessible to an audience ranging far beyond the privileged and narrow confines of the gallery art crowd … but I'm getting ahead of my narrative.

I didn't buy that issue of *Oz*, not back then. The limitations of my cash flow made even an unexpected outlay of two shillings and sixpence seem wildly reckless, and on top of this I had a strong suspicion that my parents would almost certainly go apeshit were they to discover such an openly depraved publication tucked in amongst their son's near-complete set of *The Fantastic Four*. (As it turned out, I was right. By then, however, I was taller than either of them and we worked it out.) However, even though my full immersion in the work of Crumb and the other underground cartoonists was still some months away, that cover image continued to haunt me, implying as it did a whole undiscovered world of similar delights.

My entry into that world, when it came, was accomplished with the help of a then-novel phenomenon, this being the comic shop. I realize that now the little devils are all over the place, but back in 1967–68 there was only one such establishment in the whole of England: London's Dark They Were and Golden-Eyed. As its name suggests, like many such shops of that era, it straddled the twin roles of fantasy book dealer and head shop without difficulty. Unsurprisingly then, as the first American underground comix began to filter through to this side of the Atlantic, they began to appear upon the shop's racks, or at least, under its counters.

I think the first full-length underground comix publication that I ever paid out good money for was a Dutch pirate anthology from the Real Free Press, entitled *Gung-Ho!*, which reprinted (presumably without payment, in the spirit of the times) a wide array of strips by different luminaries of the early underground scene. The book contained early work by Spain, Gilbert Shelton, Kim Deitch, and Robert Williams along with Wilson, Lynch, Griffin, Moscoso, and a host of other people who were quickly to become enduring favorites and sources of inspiration. Pride of place was given to Crumb, however, with a number of vintage pieces including the classic "Meatball" kicking off the anthology. To say that the book made a deep impression is an understatement. Phrases from it began to enter my vocabulary; weird non sequiturs that could be effortlessly inserted into the conversation of any teenage dope-and-beer party with impunity, ranging from Crumb's war cry of "Meatball!" to the immortal classicism of S. Clay Wilson's "I can't see jackshit! Got an eyeful of busted shades!"

I was hooked in the worst way, and from that point on would voraciously seek out any title to which the word underground could be applied, irrespective of its merits. Impressionable youth that I was, different favorites would wax and wane. An infatuation with the opiated stippling of Dave Sheridan would give way to an awe of the schizophrenic chrome landscapes of Robert Williams, or the flowing, shifting continuums of Victor Moscoso. Throughout it all, however, Crumb remained as the backbone of the genre, and though other artists would enthrall and fascinate me in their turn, there was always an extra edge of excitement in seeing the latest issue of *Zap*, already dog-eared, poking from the comic spinner in the darkest corner of the shop.

If Crumb's development had been arrested, if he'd stopped exactly where he was in the sixties, then he would probably still have remained a personal favorite, a time-locked slice of nostalgia to pull out and look at every once in a while. But of course he didn't stand still at all, and in that development lies, I think, his greatest triumph.

Recapping that evolution presents problems when it comes to the patchy distribution of Crumb's work over here, and I've no doubt that a Crumb historian (are there such things? I suppose so; there should be) will find lots to disagree with in the following résumé, but this is after all, a subjective work, so I'll calls 'em as I sees 'em.

Crumb's earliest work shows a youthful sense of delight and exuberance, a sense of glee to be working in the comic medium with access to all its varied icons and delights. The characters in the early pieces, however weird or

76

macabre or ridiculous, seem to be purposefully two-dimensional comic characters. Their personae, their situations, and their dialogue are all stylized to the point where they share the same slapstick territory as, say, Heckle and Jeckle. Forky O'Donnell, as opposed to being a wise-assed crow with a penchant for mischief, is an unpleasant fatboy with a penchant for stabbing people with table cutlery. His grotesque pranks are told in the same way that any animated character's more innocuous japes would be presented, right down to the sense of a winking camaraderie with the reader in the final panels. In Crumb's piece, though, the jocular presentation is belied by the violent and disturbing subject matter, turning it into something dark and different, raising all sorts of new and unsettling questions about the nature of the form itself: is the irrational violence of jabbing the prongs of a fork into someone's eyeball any more disturbing, when it comes down to it, than Jerry Mouse deciding upon a whim to crush Tom Cat's fragile skull with a weighty pig-iron bowling ball? Does Crumb's strip disturb us simply because Forky is recognizably human while Tom and Jerry, for all their obviously human traits, at least have the good taste and decorum to dress up in animal costumes before maiming each other? Whatever one's answer to these posers, the irony that sparked them off always rested in the juxtaposition of Crumb's dangerous sensibilities with his almost slavish recreation of the traditions of mainstream, knockabout juvenile humor. His people would bump their heads, see stars, say "What th—?" and gush sweat droplets when dismayed, just like cartoon characters were supposed to. Then they'd fuck their barely teenage daughter or denounce the evils of international capitalism, all without the slightest change of pace.

As the years went by, however, the thrust of Crumb's work seemed to change. This didn't happen overnight, but the appearance of strips like "Leonore Goldberg and Her Girl Commandos" seemed to indicate that the artist was leaning towards a new sort of naturalism in dialogue and storytelling, along with something that almost approached seriousness in his narrative and content. Sure enough, strips would still appear that bore all the hallmarks of the early Crumb, but there was a gradual sense, at least as I saw it, of Crumb becoming impatient or weary with simply subverting the cartoon icons of his youth. It looked as if he felt the need to grow and was looking around for territory to grow into.

Historians will almost certainly trash the following opinion by referring to some obscure transitional piece from 1972 that I've overlooked, but for my money I think Crumb found what he was looking for in the work that he produced during the midseventies for the exemplary *Arcade,* surely the best single title to grace this medium since the heyday of *Mad* itself.

I came across *Arcade* with issue #2 or #3 in 1975, this coming after a long and bleak stretch during which it seemed that there was little of any real vigor emerging from the underground, a classification that seemed to be passing away quietly and ignominiously in its sickbed. Attracted by the unusual card-covered format, the Crumb cover, and the list of contributors, I snapped it up and was blown away.

The accomplishment of Bill Griffith and Art Spiegelman in *Arcade* is considerable and deserves commenting upon at greater length than space or time will currently allow, but, briefly put, *Arcade* was perhaps the last of the original wave of underground comix, as well as their finest hour. At the same time, it managed to pave the way, with its eclecticism, for the post-underground titles of later years, including *Raw* and Crumb's own *Weirdo.* It introduced the underground comix audience, raised upon slick and capable psychedelic illustration, to what seemed like a whole new school of brilliant and startling primitives like Mark Beyer or Aline Kominsky.

As well as showcasing new and radically different artists, *Arcade* also seemed somehow to encourage work from underground artists of long standing that ranked amongst the best they'd ever done. This is true of someone like Spain Rodriguez, whose "Stalin" in *Arcade* #4 ranks as one of my favorite single comic strip pieces of all time, and it is certainly true of Robert Crumb.

In his work for *Arcade*, we see Crumb confidently striking out for new pastures with an assurance that shows in every line. Furthermore, with each passing issue of *Arcade*, Crumb's work seemed to become even stronger. I'd scarcely recovered from the hard, no-nonsense pessimism of Crumb's look at life in "This Here Modern America" when along came his powerful and affecting portrait of an early backwoods bluesman, "That's Life." This piece, which manages to chart the rise and fall of a whole section of the music industry while telling a powerful human story is, I think, one of the best things that Crumb has ever done. A sad and bitter indictment, it is nevertheless accomplished with a real human warmth.

In technical terms, Crumb's most striking work from the *Arcade* period is probably the tale of "Those Cute Little Bearzy Wearzies" from issue #6. A flat and relatively uneventful slice of low-rent life told in a hypnotic sequence of small, identically sized panels, it reads something like "Last Exit to Disneyland." The intentional monotony of its pacing, steering clear of big exciting events or dramatic resolutions, forces the reader to focus upon the simple mundane fact of the characters' lives. We see the characters' self-deceptions, their strengths and their stupidities, their fluctuating love for each other and the forlornness of their situation. Quiet and understated in a way that would typify a lot of Crumb's later work, this strip fascinated me at the time and still does to this day.

After the sad demise of *Arcade* and the collapse of the last vestiges of the original underground comix scene, I, like other Crumb admirers, found the next few years comparatively lean going, at least in terms of available output. Maybe things were different on that side of the pond, but I can only remember picking up the odd copy of *Mr. Natural*, *Zap*, or the excellent *Dirty Laundry* during this period. Fortunately, as these were fairly busy years in my own life, they seemed to flash by rapidly. The eighties and *Weirdo* were upon me in what seemed like no time at all, the new decade having apparently prompted a new phase in Crumb's work.

Reading *Weirdo* for the first time, I suffered the shock of fascinated revulsion that usually accompanies first exposure to something I'll end up hopelessly addicted to. *Weirdo* knocked me out. Not just because of Crumb's work—all the material in *Weirdo* is interesting and the vast majority of it outright wonderful. Peter Bagge, Dori Seda, Raymond Pettibon, Ace Backwords, and all the rest contributed material that fulfilled the implicit promise of *Arcade* in demonstrating that there was healthy, wriggling life beyond underground comix. As for Crumb ... well, in my opinion, he's better than ever. There's a maturity and control in the stuff he's doing now that builds upon the work that's gone before and which has been accomplished without losing any of the experimental cutting edge. The "Psychopathia Sexualis" piece; the story of Philip K. Dick's odd pentecostal visions; the sixties retrospective and the typically honest detailing of Crumb's midlife crisis; the Boswell story and the tale of Jelly Roll Morton ... shit. Until I just this moment realized that the list I was typing was getting out of hand, I never really thought about just how much extraordinary work Crumb has turned out in the last few years. I could easily add another half dozen *Weirdo* stories to the above roll call, and all of them would rank amongst the very best work that the man has ever committed to paper. How the fuck does he do this stuff?

Summing this whole rambling mess up is difficult, but if it's about anything, it's about what Crumb means to me and what growing up over the last holy-christ-surely-it-can't-be-thirty-years with Crumb's work has meant to all us holdouts from the counterculture era that it originated in. Judging from his published musings, Crumb stumbled across the midsixties in the same naive and happy state that many of us did. Like us, he got the shit kicked out of him in pretty short order. Whereas once it had seemed possible that the Whitemen governing us might be redeemed by the power of sex, suddenly all that seemed to fall to pieces. Manson and Altamont happened, both faithfully mirrored in Crumb's "Jumpin' Jack Flash." Nixon happened and we all found ourselves in the Decade of the Snoid.

The seventies, when it finally began to sink in that there wasn't going to be a last-minute cavalry charge and that what we fondly regarded as "our" culture had been almost entirely eradicated within ten years, found Crumb in a mood that reflected the times. In his *Arcade* work, it seemed that he was taking a long, hard look at the human condition and not coming away any the happier. Many of us were feeling the same thing, but only Crumb had the wit to articulate that peculiarly hollow zeitgeist, using cute bears to show us how people argue, screw, aspire, and live for no clearly defined reason or purpose; or the brief career of an itinerant blues performer to suggest that not only would the future probably be no kinder to us than the present, it would also turn us into remastered shit for the nostalgia market. There was little hope to be found in Crumb's work during this time, except in the fact that it was *there*. He was prepared to look at all the crap going down and face up to its implications. Many people his age couldn't bring themselves to do that and are now driving Porsches and working on the stock exchange.

In a similar way, although the content of *Weirdo* could never be construed as sunny and optimistic, I find it a dashingly hopeful sign in the context of its times. The slide towards despair visible in the material of the seventies did not prove terminal, for Crumb or for ourselves. Somewhere along the line that depression bottomed out, and we began to come to terms with what had happened, going on to build from there. Had the descent into the depths of pessimism been final, it seems possible that all we'd have heard from Crumb in the eighties would have been a sequence of gradually diminishing whimpers. That has not been the case. Instead, we've had a staggering array of strips united only by the grace of their accomplishment and their dizzying eclecticism. Whether recounting dreams, reminiscences, biographies of the famous, or obscure sexual histories, his latest creations indicate a man profoundly interested in the world, intent upon examining even its most remote and eccentric corners.

Certainly, the times we are currently living through are far worse than any we have personally experienced to date. I don't know if "the mean men are marching yet" over in your country, but they're certainly going for a preliminary stroll round the block over here. We are, as they say, under heavy manners—the work of Robert Crumb and other *Weirdo* contributors certainly reflecting this. However, as with *Raw*, the occasional tongue-in-cheek nihilistic posturing is belied by the simple fact that someone cared enough about something to put all of this stuff down on bristol board. Crumb's work epitomizes this more than that of anyone else I can think of. Take a look at his sketchbooks and see just how much he's capable of caring about a stack of firewood or the light on his wife's forehead or a corner of his backyard, and if that doesn't make you feel better about the world we live in, then get a friend to try holding a mirror under your nose.

Here's to you, Bob. It may be lines on paper, but it isn't *just* lines on paper. I suspect you've probably known that all along.

There's No Business by Charles Bukowski; Illustration ©1984 R. Crumb

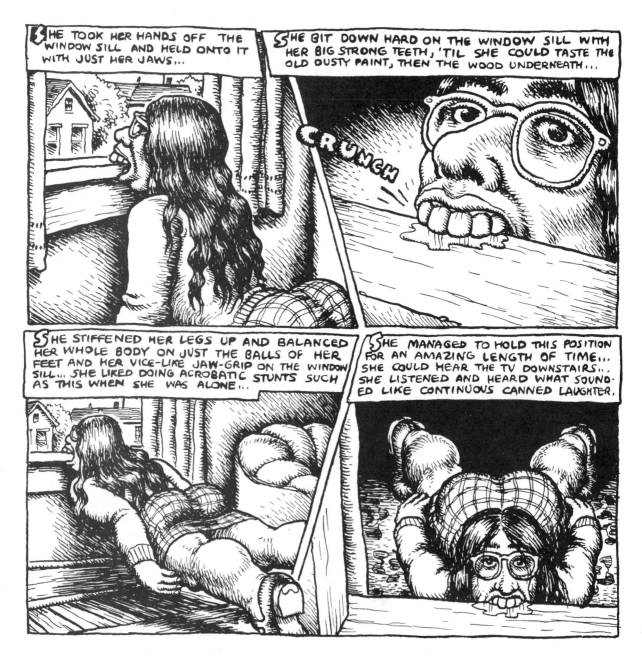

"A Gurl," *Big Ass* #2, ©1972 R. Crumb; detail

"Whiteman Meets Bigfoot," *Homegrown Funnies* #1, ©1971 R. Crumb; detail

"That's Life," *Arcade* #3, ©1975 R. Crumb; detail

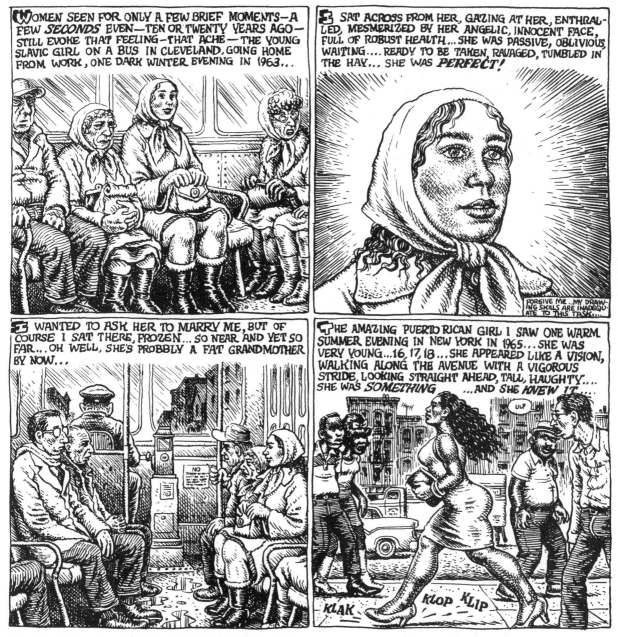

"You Can't Have Them All," *Hup* #4, ©1992 R. Crumb; detail

"Karen Meets Boz," *Weirdo* #3, ©1981 R. Crumb; detail

AS SOON AS SHE HAD DONE SO, HE RICHLY COMPENSATED HER FOR HIS NEGLECTED MARITAL DUTIES. IN THE MORNING HE SHOWED AGAIN EXTREME TENDERNESS, WHILST HE CARESSED THE WIG.

WHEN MRS. X REMOVED THE WIG SHE LOST AT ONCE ALL CHARM FOR HER HUSBAND. MRS. X. RECOGNIZED THIS AS A "HOBBY" AND READILY YIELDED TO THE WISHES OF HER HUSBAND, WHOM SHE LOVED DEARLY, AND WHOSE LIBIDO DEPENDED ON THE WEARING OF THE WIG.

REMARKABLY, A WIG HAD THE DESIRED EFFECT ONLY FOR A FORTNIGHT OR THREE WEEKS AT A TIME. IT HAD TO BE MADE OF THICK, LONG HAIR, NO MATTER OF WHAT COLOR. THE RESULT OF THIS MARRIAGE WAS, AFTER FIVE YEARS, TWO CHILDREN, AND A COLLECTION OF 72 WIGS.

CASE 110. LOVER OF FEMALE HANDKERCHIEFS; X., A BAKER'S ASSISTANT, AGED 32, SINGLE, PREVIOUSLY OF GOOD REPUTE, WAS DISCOVERED STEALING A HANDKERCHIEF FROM A LADY.

IN SINCERE REMORSE HE CONFESSED THAT HE HAD STOLEN FROM 80 TO 90 SUCH HANDKERCHIEFS. HE HAD CARED ONLY FOR HANDKERCHIEFS, AND, INDEED, ONLY THOSE BELONGING TO YOUNG WOMEN ATTRACTIVE TO HIM. HE DRESSED HIMSELF WITH MUCH TASTE. HIS CONDUCT WAS PECULIAR, ANXIOUS, DEPRESSED AND UNMANLY, AND HE OFTEN LAPSED INTO WHINING AND TEARS. HIS ANXIOUS, UNCERTAIN STATE OF MIND GAVE RISE TO A SUSPICION OF ONANISM.

THE CULPRIT CONFESSED THAT HE HAD BEEN GIVEN TO THIS PRACTICE EXCESSIVELY SINCE HIS 19TH YEAR.

FOR SOME YEARS, AS A RESULT OF HIS VICE, HE HAD SUFFERED WITH DEPRESSION, LASSITUDE, TREMBLING OF THE LIMBS, PAIN IN THE BACK, AND DISINCLINATION FOR WORK.

WITH GREAT REMORSE AND IN A WEAK-MINDED WAY, HE NOW CONFESSED THAT, AS SOON AS HE CAME NEAR ATTRACTIVE FEMALES, WITH VIOLENT SEXUAL EXCITEMENT, PALPITATION OF THE HEART, ERECTION AND *IMPETUS COEUNDI*, THE IMPULSE WOULD SEIZE HIM TO CROWD UP AGAINST THEM AND STEAL THEIR HANDKERCHIEFS.

THE MEDICO-LEGAL OPINION RIGHTLY GAVE WEIGHT TO THE CONGENITAL MENTAL ENFEEBLEMENT AND THE PERNICIOUS INFLUENCE OF MASTURBATION. THE INABILITY TO RESIST THE PATHOLOGICAL IMPULSE WAS RECOGNIZED. X. WAS NOT PUNISHED. HE HAD BUT ONE WISH; THAT SOMEONE MIGHT HELP HIM.

ON SEARCHING HIS HOUSE, 446 LADIES' HANDKERCHIEFS WERE FOUND. HE STATED THAT HE HAD ALREADY BURNED TWO BUNDLES OF THEM.

DR. MOLL WRITES CONCERNING THIS IMPULSE: THE PASSION FOR HANDKERCHIEFS MAY GO SO FAR THAT THE MAN IS ENTIRELY UNDER ITS CONTROL. A WOMAN TELLS ME; "I KNOW A CERTAIN GENTLEMAN, AND WHEN I SEE HIM AT A DISTANCE, I ONLY NEED TO DRAW OUT MY HANDKERCHIEF SO THAT IT PEEPS OUT OF MY POCKET..."

"...AND I AM CERTAIN THAT HE WILL FOLLOW ME AS A DOG FOLLOWS ITS MASTER. GO WHERE I PLEASE, THIS GENTLEMAN WILL FOLLOW ME. HE MAY BE RIDING IN A CARRIAGE OR ENGAGED IN IMPORTANT BUSINESS, AND YET, WHEN HE SEES MY HANDKERCHIEF HE DROPS EVERYTHING IN ORDER TO FOLLOW ME—I.E., MY HANDKERCHIEF."

"Psychopathia Sexualis," *Weirdo* #13, ©1985 R. Crumb; detail

D R E W   F R I E D M A N

Cartoonist: Howard Stern's Miss America, The New York Times, Spy

In 1968, when I was nine years old, the "hippest" chain of book-stores in New York City was called Bookmasters. The store, on Third Avenue between 59th and 60th (now a Crazy Eddie's), sold underground comix. It was in one of their racks that I first laid eyes on *Homegrown Funnies*, featuring the cartoons of the *greatest* cartoon genius of all times (I *really* don't want to kiss his ass), Robert Crumb. At the time I was too young to buy undergrounds, as was my twelve-year-old brother. But I *had* to own those Crumb comics. What I would do was to discreetly slip a couple of them into my father's pile of books that he was waiting to pay for in the checkout line, hoping he would just assume I was chucking a couple of *Playful Little Audrey* comic books into the pile. Little did he or any-body else realize the magnitude of the situation—that it would lead to the warping of my mind *forever*. R. Crumb's seduction of the innocent—Drew Friedman!

Early years with Crumb: As a lad, I loved the work of Crumb. It was indeed the forbidden fruit of my youth. But back then, I enjoyed all comics: *Creepy*, *Mad*, *Sick*, even superhero shit. But the undergrounds featuring R. Crumb (and Jay Lynch) were special to me, though, for several reasons: You had to be twenty-one to read them, and there I was, a mere tot, with a collection of 'em. So I was breaking the law! (Or did the dude who sold them to me break the law? Hmmmm....) Also, for a time, I became known around my school in Great Neck as the kid who would smuggle underground comix into class ... big stuff. But mainly, man, because those comics told it like it was, man, and hey, that was *far out*, man.

Copying Crumb: When that book *Steal This Book* came out in 1971, I stole about fifteen copies from Jay's Stationery Store to give out as gifts around school. Aside from that, on page 232 was a drawing by Crumb called "Stoned," featuring a bunch of folks walking around explaining to what degree they were stoned: "Sick in the head stoned," et cetera. I was drawing murals for the school library on the importance of reading for youngsters. Stuff like "Come in the library and read *The Outsiders*," with a cutesy drawing. So I drew an enlarged drawing of "Stoned" and ran block lettering over it saying "Stuff you'll see in *Steal This Book*, but not in this library." Indeed, the library did not have the book. The poster hung for about eight minutes, was taken down, and I was relieved of my library gig.

Stealing Crumb: When the film version of *Fritz the Cat* opened in 1971 I wasn't allowed to see it because it was rated X. So I took out my revenge on the Playhouse Theater by breaking in early in the morning when no one was around. It was actually pretty simple to do, just pry open the back exit door and steal the poster of the film out of the glass case in the lobby. It hung in my bedroom for a while until I realized it was Bakshi art on the poster, not Crumb. So I took it down.

Defending Crumb: When I was younger and the conversation would turn to music, I'd listen to the arguments for a while and then smugly say, "Well, there's the Beatles, then there's everybody else." One time a guy was explaining to me that Vaughn Bodé was the best cartoonist around, so I hit him with my Beatles device, tailored to Crumb. "Piff, piff," as I waved him off, "there's Robert Crumb, then there's everybody else." I could never take this guy very seriously anyway, ever since I found out he sucked on his girlfriend's toe in public.

Encountering Crumb: In 1978, having decided to be a cartoonist or something like that, I took Harvey Kurtzman's class at the School of Visual Arts. Harvey would have guests drop in from time to time. Cartoonists like Stan Mack, Jack Ziegler, Joe Orlando, etc. One day, toward the end of class, a fellow walks in followed by another guy. The first guy was a loudmouth—the guy who published *Carload o' Comics*. The other guy was R. Crumb looking *just like* R. Crumb. Crumb hugged Kurtzman. Kurtzman asked Crumb what he was doing in New York. Crumb, barely over a whisper responded, "I dunno, visiting you," and spoke no more. I, of course, found this all very thrilling and exciting and couldn't stop poking other students. "That's R. Crumb!" I'd say. One kid responded with, "Big deal, he ain't no Jim Steranko."

Concern for Crumb: For a period in the late seventies, after the demise of the great *Arcade* magazine in which Crumb had done some of his most brilliant work, it seemed to me that Crumb was going to disappear. I heard rumors that his eyesight was going; that he was going to give up drawing comics altogether to instead concentrate on seashell collages; that he was going to join the military like his father … horrible things like that. But then in 1979 came the wonderful *Best Buy Comics* followed a year or so later by *Weirdo*, and I knew everything was gonna be all right. *Whew!*

Corresponding with Crumb: I started drawing comics in 1979 and tried to get my stuff published in the usual places. I was lucky, in that I was in Art Spiegelman's class at the School of Visual Arts during the time he was starting

93

up *Raw*. He took a liking to my comics and ran some in the first issue. Crumb came out with his West Coast version of *Raw* called *Weirdo*, and I sent him a three-page strip written by my brother Josh called "The Joe Franklin Story." For some reason, I always assumed that Crumb would dislike my work; that he'd think it was too detailed, too realistic, too whatever. But to my delight, he wrote back to tell me that he did like my work and that he had been following it. Don't that beat all? You never know, do you?

Meeting Crumb: I didn't meet Crumb until 1987, at the opening of his first New York art show at the Gotham Book Mart Gallery. He looked quite the debonair figure in his tux, and as I approached and extended my hand to him, he nervously sipped his drink. "Hi Robert, I'm Drew Friedman...." We had a little chat about this and that, his toothy grin at its legendary best. But I noticed he wasn't really paying much attention to me. He was far more interested in looking around the room at the large-boned women the gallery had arranged to have there for his delight. My girlfriend later asked me how I liked meeting my favorite artist. "It was great," I said. "He didn't disappoint me."

S T E V E N   H E L L E R

Senior Art Director: New York Times Magazine

Back in the late sixties, a standing ovation at the Fillmore East was reserved for rock royalty. I was in attendance when Sly and the Family Stone was literally shouted off the stage because the audience couldn't wait any longer for Jimi Hendrix—who received the longest ovation I had ever heard. I was also there when Janis Joplin, no slouch in the ovation department, announced that the new Big Brother and the Holding Company album cover was illustrated by R. Crumb. As it was flashed on the huge screen behind her, the audience went wild.

In those days Crumb was as big as the biggest rock star. Fritz the Cat, Mr. Natural, and Keep On Truckin' had earned him icon status—they were emblems of youth culture. It's no wonder that the marriage of Janis and Crumb was greeted so excitedly. I can't tell you how many records were sold that night, but bright and early the next day I bought mine—and I still have it in relatively mint condition.

Crumb was my hero. I had been raised on *The Twilight Zone* and *Mad*, and when I saw my first Crumb comic strip in *The East Village Other* I was awestruck. I thought Wally Wood was a great comic artist, but Crumb (I couldn't believe that was his real name)—now, he was a virtuoso. The line was so pure, the gesture so perfect, the expression so emotive, and the stories—his words and pictures—were everything I wanted in a comic since I had grown out of *Mad*. They were ribald, sacrilegious, caustic, acerbic, and so damn funny I would read them aloud, and over and over.

Crumb didn't change my life, but he sure influenced it. Long after Crumb comix stopped appearing, I joined *The East Village Other* layout staff. One reason was "professional," the other was to have access to flat files that just might contain an original Crumb sketch or drawing, which I was not above borrowing for an extended period. There was a Spain, a couple of Deitches, but no Crumb. No doubt other scavengers had beaten me to it. But I did find a cache of Crumb pages from the old *EVO*, which I kept in my own personal reliquary until they, sadly, turned to dust.

Cartoonist: Eightball, Ghost World

❚ remember seeing Crumb's work for the first time in an article about underground comix in one of Steve Barghusen's father's *Penthouse*s (*Playboy*s?) sometime around 1972. There was a reproduction of the cover to *Big Ass* #1 and Steve and I were much inspired by this; so much so that we briskly set to work on our own version of *Big Ass* (about which all I remember is an "ad" I drew for the back cover which featured the headline DO YOU HAVE A BONER?). From that day on I became increasingly aware of Crumb as "the dirty cartoonist" (the first time I saw a Keep On Truckin' T-shirt [on a teen redneck in a Dog 'n' Suds in Montague, Michigan] I was sure it said Keep On *Fuckin'* and went to great lengths to keep my grandmother from seeing it), but it wasn't until I bought *Carload o' Comics* in 1978 that I began to appreciate Crumb as a masterful cartoonist first and a pornographer second. Crumb SPOKE THE TRUTH in a way that I had never seen and gave a voice to my muddled thoughts; the thoughts of another hopeless, morbidly nostalgic, overly sensitive ectomorph with a big-butt obsession. (I often wonder if these are authentic traits or if I was BRAINWASHED).

As for Crumb's work: What's not to like? He's the greatest. I especially love all the stuff he did for *Weirdo* and the four issues of *Hup*. His persistent attention to growth and improvement as an artist is a constant source of inspiration to me and any other cartoonist who's paying attention (never trust a goofball who dismisses Crumb because "he's never done a substantial graphic novel" or some such nonsense). In fact, I'll admit I'm slightly hesitant to contribute to a book like this; these things can be oppressive to a sensitive, self-conscious artiste. It's a little bit like giving him a "lifetime achievement award" or a gold watch, when I hope for nothing more than another thirty or forty years of drawing from him.

Underground Cartoonist: Choice Meats, Let's Not 'N Say We Did Funnies

In the early seventies, the Adam's Apple Distributing Company was looking for cartoonists to draw underground comix and there I was, ready and revved up to draw them. I had total freedom to do whatever I wanted: Y'wanna see naked women doing weird things? *No problem!* Y'wanna read dirty words in a comic? *Done!* Y'wanna read good stories that stick in your head? *Then read Crumb's books, okay?*

Which, of course, brings me to the Crumb "rip-off" accusations that began to plague me soon after my work started to appear. People would walk up to me and say, "Hey man, how come you ripped off Crumb's style? Huh, man? *Hah!* Fuck'n' rip-off!" This kind of reaction *really* made my day. Here I was sitting all day long busting my ass drawing these fucking comic books and what happens? A San Francisco comix dealer informs his mail order patrons that he refuses to stock "inferior" comics published by a certain company in Chicago, thereby blacklisting me. Then Crumb's wonderful lawyer decided to take advantage of these "rip-off" comix and managed to squeeze a few Gs out of my publisher, who, in turn, figured that I now owed him this money. And it couldn't have happened at a better time, since my first wife was suing me for divorce and I really needed my royalty checks.

I suppose that defending my work would be in order, but who really cares? Crumb's work did have a tremendous influence on me, but emulating it was never an intentional motive on my part. But regardless, his influence still came seeping through. The power of his work was impossible to ignore.

Crumb and I do seem to have some things in common that influenced us both. We both like 78s of jazz, blues, and hillbilly artists from the glorious twenties and thirties; early animated cartoons and funny animal comics; old toys; and Kurtzman's *Mad* ... but that's about where our similarities end. Our family and social backgrounds are as different as night and day. Whereas Crumb had trouble just talking to girls while in high school, my biggest problem was finding places to *fuck* them. Crumb was a nerd; I was trouble.

Other cartoonists emulated Crumb's self-indulgent "let's-hear-about-what-I-did-while-I-was-growing-up"storytelling style, but for my money their personal reminiscences pale by comparison. So what if these cartoonists illustrated some story about their *first* date, their *first* fuck, or the day their mother burned their comic book collection? Crumb didn't dick around with this sort of stuff. Instead, he'd do things like showing himself crawling out of his mother's womb! What kind of a person would even think about such a thing, let alone draw it? Crumb, that's who.

Making fun of anything and everything was what Crumb was all about. Nothing escaped his attention. He covered it all. While Shelton's popular dope-smoking trio, the Fabulous Furry Freak Brothers, have remained stuck in the sixties, Crumb's characters have not. Do you think that the Snoid or Fritz the Cat really gave a shit about the sixties? I don't think so. Their antics were—and still are—timeless, jack!

C H A R L E S   A L V E R S O N

Assistant Editor: Help! Magazine

When I got time to look up from the *Help!* slush pile, I couldn't help being aware that, with the departure of Gloria Steinem, the magazine was changing, losing gloss, relying less on famous names and faces. Insidiously, especially in its art—*Help!* was becoming more serious about the business of being funny. Not solemn, but serious with a capital Q, as in quality.

One of the harbingers of this trend was the appearance of "Harlem, a Sketchbook Report" by an unknown artist named Robert Crumb. As far as I know, this was his first national magazine exposure.

Stylistically, Crumb's Harlem drawings were nothing like the "hippie art" for which he was to become famous later in the sixties. Nor were they much like his second *Help!* outing, Fritz the Cat. But there was one constant. Crumb was offering, through the pages of *Help!*, his own vision of the world without having to fit into someone else's mind-set. One of Harvey's great talents was recognizing talent and letting it just *be*.

I didn't meet Crumb until more than a decade later, when I was living in Britain; during a visit to New York City, I went out to Mount Vernon to see Harvey, and he introduced me to a young, slightly gawky visitor: Bob Crumb. Terrific, I thought; now I can find out what the Great Robert Crumb is really like. And I did: Harpo Marx. Throughout my visit at Harvey's house and a long drive to New York City, Crumb did not say a single word to me. We—I realize after all these years—did not bond.

I had another chance to discover the Real Robert Crumb years later when I was asked to interview him by a seedy and slow-paying little magazine in London. This was after Crumb had retired to Winters, California, to recover from rip-off burn and learn to trust woodchucks again. Crumb was not keen on being interviewed, but I leaned heavily on our former deep relationship, and he gave in and invited me to call on him in Winters. It was not to be. After driving for what seemed like days, I realized that I was not going to be able to both get to Winters and celebrate New Year's Eve 1989 someplace where English was spoken. Regretfully, I rang him and cancelled the interview.

And there you have it: perhaps not the closest relationship, but what it lacked in depth it made up for in brevity.

Underground Cartoonist: Snarf, Lenny of Laredo, Banzai

The first place that I ever saw any of Robert Crumb's work was on American Greeting Cards, in 1962. I was living in L.A. at the time and had a nine-to-five job working for Roth Greeting Cards, and I freelanced on the side.

In 1963 Roger Brand and I went to Manhattan to stay with Larry Ivie, an avid comic book collector who lived on West 72nd Street. As I recall, it was here that Roger took me aside and showed me some early Crumb drawings that had been printed in a fanzine. Roger said that Crumb was about our age, nineteen years old, and was someday going to be a great man, as he had a rare genius.

In 1967 I got to meet Crumb, and my first impression of him was that he was shy, introverted, and acutely aware of his surroundings; sort of like a young teenager who is aware of every thought and movement and is also quite intuitive. Crumb showed me a lot of his drawings, including some of his strips that later appeared in the first

Zap. Crumb also gave me a Brannen original. His wife, Dana, was a little disturbed by this, but she let me keep it.

Both Roger and I thought of Crumb as a great artist and writer, and a true innovator of the comic book medium. I've always adored *Zap*, but I think Crumb's best work appeared in *Arcade*, which featured my favorite Crumb story, "That's Life." Other favorites include almost all of his Mr. Natural stories, especially "The Origins of Mr. Natural," in which Mr. Natural takes on many identities over the years. This particular story is very reminiscent of a Woody Allen film that came out many years later called *Zelig*. Creative people do feed off one another.

I have a Crumb comic book collection in my cartoon library. It's right next to my Walt Kelly, Frank Frazetta, Harvey Kurtzman, Ronald Searle, Carl Barks, and Albert Hurter books; and right underneath my Jack Davis original. Right where he belongs—with the *greats*!

Film Critic

Park City, Utah—"I don't ski," Terry Zwigoff was moaning. "I don't have a cellular phone. I don't have a bottle of Evian water. I don't belong here."

This was January, 1995 at the Sundance Film Festival. He looked unhappily around the bar of the Stein-Erickson Lodge, a vast hotel in the mountains above the ski resort of Park City. Cheerful skiers in Thinsulate parkas were sipping decaf cappuccinos. Zwigoff, who was wearing a beard and a sweater with animals knitted on it, shook his head.

"My movie is about a guy who was the most unpopular kid in high school. I could identify with him because I was, too. Now I come here and I feel like I'm back in high school."

We had met at the lodge to discuss *Crumb*, Zwigoff's great and astonishing new documentary about R. (for Robert) Crumb, the San Francisco underground comix artist whose style straddled the

1960s like his famous Keep On Truckin' panel. The movie, now going into national release, is *not* about underground comix. It is about the way Crumb has hung on by his fingernails to life and sanity, using art as his lifeline. *Crumb* is one of those defining experiences, like *Hoop Dreams*, like *Gates of Heaven*, that shows you how documentary films can reach parts of the human condition that fiction films don't even know about.

Zwigoff looks like vast stretches of his own human condition need first aid even as we speak. He is small, intense, with worry lines chiseled between his eyes, and although *Crumb* is an enormous hit (and would win the Sundance prize as best documentary), he almost seems to wonder if it was worth the sacrifices he made to film it.

He spent nine years on his film while averaging an income of "about two hundred dollars a month," and "living with back pain so intense that I spent three years with a loaded gun on the pillow next to my bed, trying to get up the nerve to kill myself."

The two of you must have made a great pair, I said. You were making a film about Crumb's misery while you were in greater misery.

"I think that helped. It was very hard to talk him into doing it. I had to call in every favor he owed me. We'd been friends for a while. He just wasn't interested; he doesn't like publicity."

In the film, we meet R. Crumb, his mother, his brothers Charles and Max, his wife, and various friends. We do not meet his two sisters, who wanted nothing to do with the film (one of them, Zwigoff said, has demanded "reparations" of four hundred dollars a month from Crumb for his "crimes against women"). There is a great deal about Crumb's art: his in-your-face caricatures of greedy, lustful, violent, scatological characters, flaunting their needs, perversions, and desires. There is much more about the conditions that produced it, and as we watch *Crumb* the portrait of a bizarre, dysfunctional family emerges.

There is great unease about Crumb's father, who looks terrifyingly normal in family photographs but severely punished his sons. There is a visit to the family home, occupied by Crumb's mother and by his brother, Charles—who was the first cartoonist in the family, but withdrew to permanent seclusion in an upstairs bedroom, never drawing again, or leaving the house. We also meet Max, a San Francisco monk who sits on a bed of nails, drawing a long linen cloth through his intestinal tract to cleanse it, and who is also an artist.

Crumb was obviously deeply wounded not only by his family, but by high school, where, deeply unpopular, he developed his fixation on women with hefty haunches. One of the few sources of pleasure for his male cartoon characters is riding piggyback on callipygian girlfriends; after Crumb does the same thing at a gallery opening of his work, we understand that the practice is literally, and sincerely, autobiographical.

We also learn that many of the characters who occur frequently in his drawings and comic strips are based quite closely on people he hated or lusted after in high school, and that much of his work is an elaborate process of revenge. As we get to know him and meet his family, it becomes clear that this artistic process has somehow held him together, and perhaps spared him the sort of existence that trapped his brothers.

"When I started," Zwigoff told me, "I was doing a more conventional biography of what I thought was one of the great artists of our time. But things that led in different directions ultimately shaped the film. I just kept going back to his family; maybe because I was going through this intense psychotherapy at the time. The reason I hit it off with Charles—or Robert himself, for that matter—was because I was just like those guys in high school."

It seems as if Robert's art became a way for him to deal directly with the issues in his life.

"I think the larger part of what kept Robert the saner member of the

107

family was the *success* from his artwork, not the art itself. Just getting it on paper alone in a room obviously didn't help Max or Charles too much."

Robert is always smiling, I said. It's like everything is a wry joke: *Boy, my family is crazy and weird and isn't this funny....*

"He's laughing to keep from crying," Zwigoff said.

There's one moment when he's talking about his father, and he lapses into silence, and we see this infinite sadness in his face.

"Yeah, it's where he says his father never spoke to him again after seeing one of his comics. It's a rare, off-guard moment. He's very media savvy and knows enough to keep a front on."

There are several times in the film, I said, where Robert becomes the interviewer, questioning his mother or brothers for your sake.

"He was very helpful to me in that way. But there were other times he was completely uncooperative and seemed to be trying to sabotage the film. I had known him for a long time, and we had played in this same crummy band together. After he agreed to the film, I said the only way I really wanted to do it was by including Charles and Max and his mother.

"I'd met them in the early 1970s. I was traveling with him to New York and he said, 'Why don't we just pull over and stay at my parents' house? I haven't seen them in a couple years. Would you mind spending a night there?' I spent this incredibly memorable night at their house talking to Charles and his mother, and really liked them a lot, and I always thought it would be no film without them. Of course I had no idea at that point how *much* they would figure into the film.

"So when we started the film, Robert called them on the phone. They remembered me, they liked me, so yeah, okay, they'd do the film, you know, whatever. So a couple of months later I hired a crew and we got to the motel and his mother said no, she wouldn't film. He went over there and couldn't get a real answer out of her. We were in this motel room for four days. Finally I talked to her all day and she sort of warmed up and said, 'Okay, okay—but you can only do Charles upstairs in his room.' So we filmed him and we're coming down the stairs and my cinematographer, Maryse Alberti, a Frenchwoman, says, 'Terry, we must film the mother.' I said I asked her like a hundred times; she doesn't want to be filmed. 'Let me place the light. We will just start filming her.' She throws up this light and his mother is really angry and cursing us and screaming.

"I said, 'Take the light down and let's just go; leave her alone.' 'No, no, we just do it.' So as soon as she turns the camera on his mother, she says, 'Oh, well, it's too late now; I'm in the movie.' And she really got into it."

The scenes upstairs in Charles's bedroom are among the most haunting in the film. Literate, intelligent, and even amused by his own predicament, he has a stack of battered paperbacks, which he reads and rereads, and in a closet there is artwork from his brief productive period in his teens. He talks about his lifelong obsession with the 1950 version of the film *Treasure Island* and its young hero, played by Bobby Driscoll, who in a sense represents all of the daring that the agoraphobic Charles was never able to muster.

"The one night we spent at his house," Zwigoff said, "two blocks away, the local movie theater, which had been there since they were kids, was playing *Treasure Island* on a rerelease. Robert was trying to talk Charles into going and Charles was going through this unbelievable dilemma. He didn't want to leave the house but he was dying to see this movie again. Robert said, 'Look, me and Terry will walk you over there. We'll sit with you; we'll bring you back.' He couldn't leave the house."

The film was "technically" shot between 1985 and 1991, Zwigoff said, "but there's a period there, about 1986 through 1988, where my back was so bad I was in bed most of the time, suicidal." While filming was going on, Crumb's reputation was continuing to grow, nourished by the current popularity of comics and graphic novels about Generation X, and the boom in 1960s art among collectors. Shortly after principal photography was finished, Crumb, his wife and their daughter Sophie moved permanently to the south of France.

"Sophie's eleven now," Zwigoff said. "She's directed her first film; a ninety-minute film, feature length. She wrote it, she cast it, she shot it. I asked Robert if it's any good and he said, 'I don't speak a word of French. I can't tell if it's any good.' But he said that technically it's amazing. There are these long, sophisticated tracking shots. He said she studies *Touch of Evil* on videotape, and is a very happy, well-adjusted kid."

Are they happier over there?

"He seems to be happier than I've ever known him. He's coming to the States in May. For some bizarre reason he agreed to go on the Garrison Kiellor show. We have this pretty terrible band that we've had for years, called the Cheap Suit Serenaders, and agreed to go on this show, you know. Turned down the Letterman show and all these other things, but radio was okay."

He doesn't seem too concerned about making a lot of money or becoming famous with his art.

"He was offered, like, millions to license the Keep On Truckin' drawing for Toyota, but they wanted that one drawing. He wanted to sell them a lot of other stuff. He tells them, 'How about I have this girl with her head cut off being stuffed into the trunk of the Toyota?' When they didn't go for that, he turned them down."

What happened to R. Crumb's brothers, Charles and Max, after the filming of the documentary? The following is a spoiler; read no further until you've seen the film, where some developments come as dramatic revelations.

For Charles, life in the upstairs bedroom grew increasingly pointless, and eventually he took his own life.

"He saved up an overdose of his medication to kill himself," Zwigoff told me. "Robert called me up to tell me that Charles had killed himself. I was very upset, but Robert just sorta said, 'Well, he was good as dead anyway.' Real callous about it. But later I talked to somebody who happened to be staying at his house when his mother called him and told him. And I asked, 'How did he react when that phone call came in?' And he said, 'He acted like he didn't care, but then I heard him all night long. He went up to his studio and he was pacing all night.' "

"Charles was the guy he was closest to in the entire world; the one who really shaped his whole sense of humor and his art. It was a big, devastating blow to him. And yet, he was right: Charles was sort of dead already."

After Charles died, his mother destroyed all of his artwork and the elaborate journals that are seen in the film, before Robert could rescue them.

What's the follow-through story on Max?

"Max isn't doing too well. He called me from the hospital a couple of months ago. He'd lost about forty pounds and he had weird nervous damage to his legs."

Probably from sitting on that bed of nails.

"No, it's actually a vitamin deficiency. The doctors theorize he had this severe deficiency of Vitamin B_{12}. He has these crazy theories of diet and nutrition, so they got him all screwed up, but they were getting him better by giving him vitamin injections and he eventually left the hospital. You know, in the film ... I didn't even touch the surface on Max."

HEY HEY HEY...

Zap's First Publisher

The first strip of Crumb's I saw was in an underground newspaper from Cleveland or somewhere in the Midwest. Doug Blazek, who was later at *Zap* #1's party, had a copy. He put out a little mag called *Open Skull* and published a lot of Bukowski's work. This was still before Bukowski was well known and no one in San Francisco was aware of Crumb. Underground comix didn't exist.

I had a printing press in the Mission District at the time. I liked the posters in the head shops that were beginning to do business in the Haight. I didn't care much for the religious and "Flower Age" drawings in the *Oracle*, so I put out a couple of issues of a newspaper I called *The Last Times*, and lifted the Crumb strip. There was a need for more papers that the street kids could hawk, so someone was there buying all I could print, which was only one hundred to five hundred or so copies. I never made any money on it.

I was into the literary, cinema, and later, the music scene at the time Crumb came to San Francisco. I had kept an old prewar Multilith and off-set camera from the Mission shop. We began throwing nude parties at our new Post Street address. Someone at City Lights Bookstore had given us complimentary tickets to the Janis Joplin and Big Brother concert, but we were too stoned to get there, though it was only a few blocks. Lots of people were dropping by our Post Street flat—someone talking about a new group he was involved with called Pink Floyd; Billy Jharmark of the Batman Gallery, who later gave me his '52 MGTD Classic, and his friend, Bob Branaman, who was living in the backseat of his '49 Chevy. Even Huncke visited us at that pad and we associated him with the disappearance of an IBM Selectric, bless his heart. There was junk on the street and pot in the cupboard.

Bob Branaman was a "finder." He eventually turned up everyone who was anyone. It was one of his business deals, or as close as one could come to it, that brought Don Donahue to the door.

It was supposed to be five thousand copies, but that's a stretch. I'll tell you why. But first—I loved the drawings Don laid out on the desk. I felt like a kid, curled up again in a big armchair reading the old famous comics, so I knew these drawings were important artworks and I wanted to be identified as the printer, so I stipulated that my name should appear on the bottom of the back cover.

The creation of a comix scene belongs to Don Donahue, who later took my press for a little cash and a tape recorder. He said he knew something about printing, but it seemed as though he knew only a little about graphic arts, maybe prepress experience. I had to send him back to Crumb to explain that he had to draw each color for the cover as a separate image, to overlay, to fit like a piece of a puzzle. We certainly didn't have color process capabilities with a prewar Multilith and a press camera in the bathroom. Hence, the format that I had to work with, and that Don continued with for some time as the comix format, was adopted because that's all the size we could get out of a small printing press. I would have to make the five-hundred-dollar Multilith dance and sing.

I took on the job. But it was the lack of technology that made the count of completed copies much lower. Most everyone there was on acid or pot and was so excited to see the finished copy that I don't know who counted.

Prior to that meeting, I had been attending parties at Don Allen's, who was the West Coast editor for Grove Press. I tried to get both him and Ferlinghetti to publish Crumb, and having a hunch just how great Keep On Truckin' was, I had Crumb almost ready to give it to me—but he had to do something else with it. The literary publishers seemed uninterested in Crumb at the time. I was later paid well (three hundred dollars plus, each) for a couple of poems that were illustrated in *Evergreen Review* by artists I never knew; I tried to introduce publishers to Crumb, but they had other interests (or tastes).

Anyway, we completed the job and went to Crumb's apartment for a party. We got high and drank and ate cake with frosting. I had been around enough beginnings to know that something was happening; fame was in the air, and with fame, more pussy. I thought to myself that this might be his wife's last taste of that cake's frosting. I especially remember the overstuffed armchairs and his old Philco radios.

The collector's item "Printed by Charles Plymell" is well worth its price because its count was short. The last one I saw I had given to a friend's kid who lived on the Bowery. He used to take it down to the Bat Cave in the city and watch its value climb....

It was many years later, while living in Cherry Valley, that S. Clay sent word of a comix show in the city. I hadn't seen Crumb since the first *Zap*, nor S. Clay since I printed his first folio on Grist's press when I was working at the Campbell's pork and bean factory in Lawrence, Kansas. The plan to go to this show began the strange comixesque episode in Cherry Valley with a local character straight out of a sixties cartoon—a seventies comics fan, mechanic, dreamer, "Dangerous" Dan; his friend, Ray; Mike, myself, and Melodie. Ray had an old four-door Caddy with a Bat Signal painted on the back (he went in for a revival fad at the time).

The line at the gallery was several blocks long. I caught a glimpse of Spain, who got us in, but it was packed so much I couldn't get to S. Clay. Crumb came out and talked to Ginsberg. I tried for a photo but the camera lens was all wet from sweat. I gave it to Melodie, who tried to get some shots. I squeezed my way to Crumb to say hello and talked to Ginsberg for a while. People started asking me for my autograph and took pictures I've never seen. Ginsberg turned to me and gestured to the packed gallery and said, "See what you started."

The rest of the evening was spent trying to press in to see S. Clay, but we had to leave. On the way home, we were stopped by New Jersey troopers who demanded that Ray, in his baseball cap, get out of the car. He handed them a temporary license, which made the trooper snarl, "What's this, your kindergarten report card?" One by one we filed out of the car while they searched the trunk. They were sure they had something … but what? Finally, I, a white-bearded old man wearing a handkerchief around my head, got out and told the troopers that I was from a small village which didn't have many resources and Ray was the only limo driver I could find. They sensed the paperwork would be too much on this scene, so they told us to keep on going … out of New Jersey. There was a lot more to that cartoon, waiting. It does seem, though, that reality does a special twist when it is near a comic … er … a cosmic event.

I hear that Crumb got some heat from the multicultural fems about his ladies with the big butts and the like. He has chosen to live in France. I think that's a good idea. The best way to really see this country, if it isn't in a cartoon, may be from far away.

116

E   R   I   C   S   A   C   K

Underground Art Collector

As I sit down to write this essay, the Dow Jones average pokes at 10,000; Leonardo da Vinci's *Codex Leicester* has sold for $32 million; a single United States coin has sold for over $1 million. So why does it amaze and impress me when Robert Crumb's original drawings sell for $1,000, $10,000 and *over* 50,000 U.S. smackeroos!?!

Ah, yes ... I remember my high school daze in the late sixties and early seventies. A dear friend lent me a comic he just got numbered zero. *Zero!* Who ever heard of such a thing? Crumb's cover totally "zapped" me, enticing me to fold back its cover and discover the graphic tale that would change my conscience and art appreciation (as well as keep me laughing) *forever*: "Meatball." In order to feed my habit for these "new kind" of funny books, I became sort of a school distributor—buy four copies, sell three, and mine was *free!*

Around 1980, I attended The New York Comic Con—a spectacular event with energy that could be felt the second you walked in. In the back of the room was a dealer with the original art to an S. Clay Wilson story from *Zap* and a Crumb serial page from the *Village Voice*. The richness of these pages in their *original* full size was captivating. The three pages set me back $800 (figuring about two for the Crumb), a huge sum for me in those days, albeit the first of many originals I would later acquire.

Fortunately (or unfortunately when I'm in hot pursuit of a piece), this passion for Crumb originals is now shared by many. These folks, like myself, who enjoyed his work in their youth have become mature and of means, and now desire to own a piece of the "magic." Since the beginning of Sotheby's comic art auctions, Crumb art has been present and has commanded very respectable sums. Pieces that were available earlier for a couple of hundred dollars now sell in the $1,500 to $7,500 range.

In 1993 a Madison Avenue gallery presented a show of Crumb's work in a setting so elegant that, if they could, it would cause the images themselves to blush. The originals were hung in handsome frames, illuminated to ideal standards, and accompanied by an expensive hardbound catalog allowing those interested to have images never seen before. This newfound appreciation in Crumb's work has brought about an interesting phenomenon: his most classic pieces from the early *EVO*, *Zap*, and *Head Comix*, long thought to have been lost to the counterculture and its cannabis-clouded "free spirit," have emerged, and in spectacular condition! They show all the hunger, passion and social sarcasm that made Crumb the great, and now appreciated, artist that he is. Some of these very pieces command prices ranging from $5,000 to *over* $50,000(!!!).

What the future will bear, no one knows. Will the French government acquire even more Crumb art for *their* museums? Will there become a greater U.S. appreciation for this American resource encouraging our *own* museums to offer these works to the public? Will a Crumb original surpass the *Codex Leicester* in value?

Remember folks, it's only lines on paper....

Underground Cartoonist: The East Village Other, Arcade, Raw, Zero Zero

It isn't as if there wouldn't have been an underground comix movement without Crumb. He didn't invent underground comix. I know that for a fact, because I and a few other people I know were already drawing them in underground newspapers before we were really aware of Crumb. But even knowing that, it still almost seems as if he did, so great is the impact he's had.

I first really became aware of his work in an underground newspaper from Philadelphia called *Yarrowstalks*. Later I realized I'd seen a few smatterings of his work several years earlier in Harvey Kurtzman's *Help!* magazine. But at the time that I saw *Yarrowstalks* #1, I didn't connect him with the earlier stuff.

The first *Yarrowstalks* appeared in the late spring or early summer of '67. I was already a published veteran of some months, and I was doing a strip called *Sunshine Girl* for an underground paper known as *The East Village Other*. I wasn't getting any regular pay, but it wasn't really a major injustice. This strip was strictly beginner stuff. There were a couple of Crumb strips in that issue of *Yarrowstalks*, and I remember liking them enough to buy a copy. One of the strips featured Mr. Natural and I remember being shocked because he said the word *fuck*. The only thing terribly remarkable about it was that I'd never seen it done before in a comic strip. I was also vaguely disturbed by how well this Crumb guy drew. "Pretty good," I mused. That's all these strips were, pretty good, but legitimately so. And what I was to quickly find out was that I literally didn't know the half of it.

A short time later, a third issue of *Yarrowstalks* appeared. Crumb did the cover, the logo, and a number of good comic strips and illustrations inside. It was all great stuff, but I still hadn't seen the whole of it in terms of the scope of this man's talent. Nevertheless, it seemed impressive enough then. And that particular issue of *Yarrowstalks* was about to have a bigger impact on my own situation than I ever realized when I bought it.

About three nights later, I walked into the office of *The East Village Other.* It was pasteup night, so I was sure of finding the man I'd come to see: Walter Bowart, the publisher. My strips were then allotted half a page in *EVO* (as the paper had come to be called), but in the last two or three issues, I'd been craftily increasing their length, making them larger by increments. I'm sure that sounds kind of silly, but the first time I'd asked for a whole page, the editor said yes, then turned around and printed my strips smaller yet, just slightly larger than a vertical postcard. Anyway, I'd decided that sneaking my way to more space was really an ineffectual strategy. My purpose in going to see Bowart was to make my pitch for an officially sanctioned three-quarters of a page.

I found Bowart in galvanic action, supervising the last minute putting-together of the latest *EVO*. All the pages that were ready hung in a long row with occasional spaces awaiting pages that were still being worked on. Bowart listened as I made my case. I followed him around as he moved rapidly here and there, supervising last-minute details. It hardly seemed as if he was listen-

120

ing. But he certainly had been, for when I finished my spiel he said, "Draw me some strips like this and I'll give you a whole page!" I looked to where his hand was pointed and to my great surprise we were standing in front of a full-page Crumb comic strip, one that I had just seen in *Yarrowstalks*, hanging up and ready to go into the next issue of *EVO*. Bowart raved on about at last having found the perfect acid-head cartoonist, but I scarcely heard him. I was stunned.

Soon the money I'd come to New York City with was running low, and my no-pay gig at *EVO* was getting old. I was having some personal problems, and I started drinking more and getting flakier in general, and I stopped drawing comic strips altogether. I started getting work out of seedy employment agencies that handed out daily menial jobs, mostly to bums. It was depressing. I seemed to be rapidly becoming a bum myself! Then I made a lot of radical changes in my life. I started taking yoga lessons in a place run by a swami with a long gray beard and a bright orange gown. I quit drinking. I got a good-paying civil service job at the post office. I even started taking art courses at Pratt Institute's night school. It was an odd time. I gradually became rather calm and responsible, even kind of happy. But not terribly creative.

Walter Bowart quit somewhere around this time, and the paper got worse. But I continued to read every issue for one main reason: Crumb.

Crumb had responded to the enthusiastic reception of his work by sending in a big pile of new strips. They were greater by even larger leaps than any of his work I'd seen till then. Even though his work had had the initial effect of undermining my confidence as an artist, these new strips were so damned good that I couldn't help enjoying them. I was turning into an enthusiastic fan in spite of myself. More than a fan, really. I just loved those early strips. The effect they had on me, in terms of showing the way to further possibilities of the comic strip medium, is hard to describe. They simply blew me away.

One afternoon I stopped by the *EVO* office. They'd been running an ad for me that offered buttons with a picture of my character Sunshine Girl on them, and I came by to pick up the latest orders. Even though my strip was no longer running, orders for my buttons still dribbled in. While there, I was waylaid by the paper's new boss. He was an ex-CPA named Joel Fabricant, sometimes known as Jay Fab. The contrast between Joel and his predecessor was marked, to say the least. Bowart was a slick, jivey, flower-power kind of guy. Joel on the other hand was a rough, crude person who didn't read *EVO*, voted Republican, and only seemed jivey until you got to know him. There was a disconcertingly blunt honesty in him that came across almost immediately.

Still, I didn't know what to think as he ushered me into his office. He was rather hyper, speaking in loud, impatient staccato bursts. He offered me a cigarette, which I refused, and went into his pitch. What it boiled down to was this: they'd run out of Crumb strips. He was aware that *EVO*'s quality was slipping, and he'd noticed the trickle of mail that I was still getting and wanted me to start doing comic strips for *EVO* again.

I wasn't ready for this. I'd gotten used to my newly adjusted life and good-paying job. So I started to tell him that I really didn't think that I wanted to come back, but Joel wouldn't take no for an answer. He again offered me a cigarette and told somebody to send Spain in. I'd known Spain for about a year. He was already at *EVO* doing illustrations for no pay when I first started there. As soon as Spain came in, Joel began describing Spain's current position at the paper. He was doing a weekly, full-page strip, along with other illustrations as they were needed, and helped out in other ways. For this, he received forty dollars a week. That may not seem too sensational, but in 1968, the prospect of getting a guaranteed salary for doing comic strips seemed like a miracle to me. I still think of it as a miracle, even now. And there were fringe benefits. Joel paid for our art supplies, and we had free drinking privileges at a club called the Steve Paul Scene, located uptown.

Yes, I was soon drinking again, too. I'd gotten mugged around this time and now carried a loaded pistol in my jeans. And as much as I'd benefited from yoga, it just didn't seem to fit in anymore. I'd become a hard-drinking, comic-drawing fool.

Working for Joel was a real experience. Superficially, he was a crude loudmouth who could and would kick ass when necessary. He was also as good as his word in a deal and, I think, a fundamentally decent man.

One week, a review was picked up from somewhere and run in *EVO* for a new comic book by Crumb. It was *Zap* #1, and two pages from it ran with the review, which also included an address where, for twenty-five cents and a dime for postage, a copy could be obtained. I sent for one immediately. A while later, it arrived. To my delight, Crumb had drawn a small picture on the envelope of my character, Sunshine Girl, cracking up while reading a *Zap*. Well, what's there to say about *Zap* that hasn't been said before? It was, and still is, a great comic book; the first of many from one of the great masters of the medium.

It was perhaps six months later when I actually got to meet Crumb. I was up in my Eighth Street slum working on my weekly strip when Spain, who was now my roommate, came in—and Crumb was with him! I was so startled that I could barely speak, but did manage to stammer out something about how much I loved his work. Crumb turned out to be an all-around good fellow, decidedly upbeat in those days. He was traveling with a small ukulele-sized banjo at the time, and he'd occasionally grab it up and start singing a snatch of some old popular song at the drop of a hat. He was clean shaven and even had longish hair. It was as close as he ever came to looking like a hippie. He crashed with us for a couple of days, and he had one of his perennial sketchbooks with him. It was a treasure trove of spontaneous, brilliant, entertaining art. I was floored. He showed us Xeroxes of a comic he'd done prior to *Zap* #1, which was meant to be the first *Zap*, but the original art had been lost somehow. If anything, it was an even greater book than *Zap* #1. Floored again!

Soon Crumb was up at *EVO*, turning out comics along with me and Spain, and you'd better believe Spain and I were busting our asses! There was

123

a lot of internal turmoil going on around that time. Ex-publisher Walter Bowart was back in town. He'd originally left *EVO* for Arizona to marry a rich girl—Andrew Mellon's granddaughter, I believe—but I guess the easy life was starting to bore him, because once again he was trying to take over at *EVO*.

I forget the details, but there was reason to believe he had the legal clout to do it. What's more, he was making big noises about doing some house cleaning, and the raunchiness of our comic strips had been mentioned as one of the things in need of correction. Well, damn few people at *EVO* wanted Walter back. One could say what one would about Joel, but he'd put *EVO* on a sound business basis and given us salaries we could count on. Bowart was a guy who promised much and wasn't too reliable.

He'd been back for about a week, and anti-Bowart feelings were running high. I got so worked up that I drew a comic strip attacking Bowart, which I intended to get into the next issue of *EVO*. I got Spain, Crumb, and Trina to draw little cameos in this strip. On pasteup night Bowart, who'd heard about the strip, confronted me and asked to see it. I was kind of drunk, and I showed it to him with alcoholic bravado. Walter laughed heartily at the strip, but he wasn't laughing for very long because before I knew what had happened, I was practically screaming at him. I called him every name in the book. It was eerie. All week long everybody had been loudly bad-mouthing Walter. He was being cursed out in every conceivable way behind his back, but now, during my showdown with him, it was just me and him. I wasn't sure whether I'd blown my job or not, so I told Crumb about it the next day, and he just slapped his knee, as he does, and laughed. Luckily for me, it was pretty apparent soon afterwards that Bowart was giving up his takeover attempt.

A month or so later, Crumb drifted back to his home base in San Francisco. He left his banjo-uke behind with Spain as proof that he'd be back. It was becoming increasingly apparent that the real future of underground comix was in San Francisco. Early in '69, I made a brief pilgrimage there with my girlfriend, Trina Robbins. Crumb was in Detroit at the time drawing *Motor City Comics*, but his wife, Dana, invited us to stay at their place in the Haight. Spain was in the midst of a long visit out there and I looked him up. I also met such legendary characters as Rick Griffin, S. Clay Wilson, Rory Hayes, Gary Arlington, and Don Donahue. The atmosphere was exciting, to say the least! I started drawing comics for various publications right away. About two and a half weeks later we returned to New York, but I vowed that I'd be back.

No sooner was I back than I was knee-deep in publishing comics. Vaughn Bodé had been editing a tabloid-sized comic called *The Gothic Blimp Works* for Joel. I'd already been dubbed one of his assistants even before my trip, but the hippie life was catching up with Vaughn. At the time, he was superficially a rather prim fellow, and now, after two issues, he was bailing out. Before I knew what happened, I was editor and under blunt instructions from Joel to get more work from Crumb. This was a problem. Crumb had actually been in on the early planning of the *Blimp* and even drew the first two covers. But he had argued hard for doing the publication in a standard-sized comic book format. *EVO* had published a tabloid-sized comic before, in 1967, called *Zodiac Mind Warp*, but it had been such a flop that a follow-up tabloid comic I had drawn the same year never got published. When Crumb's arguments for the smaller format was overruled by Joel and Bodé, his interest faded. For my first issue as editor, I did manage to get Crumb grudgingly to do a cover. And I schlepped along. We actually weren't doing all that badly with the *Blimp*. But I still had California fever and I was privately making plans to move there.

Crumb turned up in New York again in the summer of '69 in a wild and crazy mood. He was feeling his oats, full of enthusiasm for the future and drawing better than ever. Meanwhile, one underground comic after another started coming out of San Francisco. Some were good and some were awful, but it was clear that the boom was on. How clear? Well, I'll tell you. As 1969 dwindled, and Trina and I prepared for our San Francisco adventure, the same thing was happening with underground comic artists all over town. During the next six months, most of them had trekked to California in what seemed like a mass migration—like lemmings marching to the sea.

I parted with *EVO* on good terms, and they continued sending me copies out in California. Crumb continued his nomadic travels, turning out great comics wherever he went. Perhaps nine months after I left, he again turned up in New York, and shortly thereafter, his art appeared on the cover of an issue of *EVO*. But it was the cover of the next week's issue that I'll never forget. It featured a photo of Joel Fabricant with fresh pie dripping from his face, looking like he was about to kill somebody. There were more photos inside, and one of them showed the thrower of the pie: Robert Crumb. Secondhand, I heard that Joel had called a meeting and was evidently waxing obnoxious. I don't know the exact details. But Crumb *did* pitch the pie, and Joel *didn't* kick Crumb's ass. Not long afterward, Joel quit *EVO* and I honestly don't know how much, if anything, the pie-throwing incident had to do with it. But something was eating at him. Joel did make an odd remark when he left. Now, this is a man who literally was heard to say many a time, "My god is the dollar." But as he left *EVO*, it is said that someone heard him mutter that maybe money really *wasn't* everything. Later, I heard that *EVO* was briefly owned by John Lennon and Yoko Ono. But I don't know if that's really true. I do know that it didn't survive past Joel's regime by much.

In summing up Crumb's influence, I have to say that it is hard to measure. It goes far beyond the brilliant quality of his own work over the years. He's set such a consistently high standard that it's had the effect of also spurring others on to greater efforts. What's more, again and again he has gone well out of his way to encourage and help his fellow artists. What more could one hope for in the leader of an artistic movement? He is a giant in the contemporary world of art, and I consider it a high privilege indeed to often have my work appear in print with his, and to know him.

D A N A   C R U M B

First Wife of Robert Crumb

When Robert was nineteen years old he left home for Cleveland, Ohio, an apartment with weird Marty Pahls, and a bleak job at American Greeting Cards.

Lonely, love-starved, painfully shy, he passed the long winter nights creating a fantasy and entitled it *R. Crumb's Big Yum Yum Book*.

One afternoon with an ever-so-faint hint of spring in the air, my friend Liz called me to come over to her place to see this amazing work of art and meet the young artist. "What the hell?" I said. Anything to get away from my horrible mother and, after all, it *was* beginning to be spring.

I sat down on a pillow in Liz's front room and read the *Yum Yum Book* cover to cover. It took me about an hour to fall in love with Robert Crumb.

Then I met him.

He was walking up the old worn marble stairs, scrollwork

iron banisters and all, and I was walking down. I, thank God, was already in love, because the first glimpse of Robert in those days was quite arresting. The word *geek* was not in vogue, so let's just say that Crumb was quite a trendsetter. It was lust at first sight. I loved him even more upon sight than I had moments earlier after looking at his work. I saw one of my unborn children staring at me through his eyes and thus our journey together began.

We spent a lot of time together. Lost our virginity together. At first, I would go to his and Marty's apartment after school and make dinner for them. Marty ate the dinners and between mouthfuls warned Crumb that I was out to trap him. My parents finally busted me after a weekend with Robert and kicked me out.

One thing led to another and we were married on September 11, 1964. The wedding was sad and silly. My father got us a really cheesy room at the Statler Hotel, which had old brown gardenias on the fire-escape window. Much as I thought I loved him, I spent my wedding night mostly in tears. I had been a very intuitive child—on that September night, I became a very intuitive adult. There were to be many more nights of tears. Also days of joy and moments of great happiness.

We moved to New York and lived in my aunt Leah's Lincoln Center apartment for about four or five weeks while we made plans to go to Europe and live there for as long as we could on our savings, the money gleaned from returning all of our wedding presents.

We booked passage on a Norwegian freighter with eight other passengers and off we went. Big dreams and scared shitless.

We spent about nine months walking all over Europe. Harvey Kurtzman sent us to Bulgaria for ten days. Let me tell ya, folks, Bulgaria in 1964 was quite a trip for two silly pigeons. Quite a trip, indeed.

We came back to the States via Iceland Airlines—kinda the Continental Trailways of the sky.

Robert was always leaving me and then coming back, or capitulating and allowing me to come along.

We stayed in Cleveland awhile, then moved to New York City. We both thought we had jobs. We didn't. There were good times in New York, and sad. We had a one-room apartment about three floors up and Crumb and I both did a lot of work for Woody Gellman at Topps Chewing Gum and Nostalgia Press. Woody was always giving us huge boxes of fresh bubble gum. One day, while our dear friend Per Bjierfjord was living with us, we got the brilliant idea to throw wrapped gum out the window onto First Avenue at 83rd Street and see what people would do. It became one of our greatest forms of entertainment. Hell, we were poor and bored! You know, people would pick up the gum; step on and around the gum; look around; look at one another. Seldom, if ever, did people look up.

After moving to San Francisco and living in Haight-Ashbury, we used to like to try to give away spare change and could seldom, if ever, get people to take it from our open palms.

Living in the Haight was fun! I liken it to living during a renaissance period in America. We met a lot of people and a good time was had by all.

When the first *Zap Comix* came out, Marilyn Jones (McGrew), Robert, Don Donahue, and I sat on our apartment floor collating, folding, and stapling it. Then I would go up to Haight Street and sell them out of a baby carriage. I was very pregnant and continued my route with baby Jesse in that same carriage after he was born. One day while delivering comix to various shops on Haight Street, Bobby Bowles came tripping out of his store, The Boot Hook, saying "What do you have? Oh look! It's a ten-pound boy and a bunch of comic books!"

In 1969 we got some money from Ballantine Books. Jesse was almost a year old and I really wanted to raise him in the country. So we journeyed forth and found our home in Potter Valley. We were happy off and on. The first year was hard. We gathered wood at the local sawmill daily to stay warm. In the spring, Robert worked the soil for our first garden, and friends often came for visits to the country. But it was also the beginning of our ending.

Robert and his girlfriend, Aline, moved away and my children and I stayed here. My sons Jesse and Adam were raised here at "Camp Dana." Robert and I went through some bitter times and then the divorce.

I saw him for a few days in the summer of 1996 and realized that I still had love in my heart for him. Or at least a very special place in my heart for him. I believe it will be there always, that special place.

Unless, of course, he fucks with me....

Underground Comix Writer: Deviant Slice, Legion of Charlies

Straight Arrow Press, the book publishing arm of *Rolling Stone*, was run by a smooth and sophisticated New York editor whose name I've conveniently forgotten. (Although I could look it up in our politely angry correspondence, which I still have.) This man agreed to pay some bucks to Mark James Estren for an anthropology/history of underground comix, but only if the underground artists would let their work be reprinted for free.

As I was told by Estren, Robert Crumb wouldn't accept such an arrangement, so Straight Arrow made a separate deal with Crumb. They couldn't do the book without him, seeing as he had invented underground comix.

They sent out engraved cards to everybody else, inviting us to a big "preview party" in North Beach, with promises of lots of liquor and eats. Liquor there was, in abundance, but the centerpiece of the party was a fat mock-up of the proposed "history." We were all invited to go through it and see how famous we were all going to be once Wenner & Company had bestowed their imprimatur upon us. The New York editor and Estren circulated through the crowds cornering people individually and getting them to sign "releases." When the question of payment would come up, they would mumble something like, "Yeah, a book like this is highly risky. If we go into a second printing, there will be some money." But no written promises were made.

Now, it's well known that the undergrounders were a feisty and revolutionary lot, but the slicks hit 'em quick and hard that night. With few exceptions they caved in, one and all, to the charms of the "overground" press lords. The exceptions were, to the best of my knowledge: S. Clay Wilson and Greg Irons—and to the extent that I collaborated with Greg, myself.

For Greg it was an especially painful moment. Estren planned to appropriate huge amounts of Irons art: no less than fifty-seven pages of his "history." Several complete stories were to be reprinted, including "Vince Shazam," from *Deviant Slice* #2 and the GI/TV autobiographical classic "Last Gasp," from *Slow Death* #5.

So they sat Greg and me down with drinks and eats and offered us "releases" to sign. And we politely said, "No way." Then we attempted to "negotiate" asking for what we thought was a very reasonable page rate and a small return from all future printings.

Estren, let it be said, wanted to pay everybody. But the dope-smoking Boy Scouts at Straight Arrow were having none of it. They told us point-blank, "Either you sign or you're out of the history of underground comix."

How ironic! Here we were going to be drummed out of the history of our own work by the very people we considered the "enemy"—the hip media bosses from *Rolling Stone*. What a joke!

I haven't looked at Estren's crippled "history" since it first came out, but if you'll go through it yourself, I don't believe you'll find a single scrap of Greg

Irons's work, unless they found something they could reprint because Greg forgot to put a copyright symbol on it. Wilson, I believe, is represented by one or two little pieces that were ripped off under exactly those circumstances: some little mag he gave some art to forgot to print a copyright notice.

Estren replaced Greg's pages with a lot of miscellaneous junk, including pages from my brother Rick's *Two-Fisted Zombies*, which I cowrote. Rick was young and hungry for exposure, and neither Greg nor I wanted to force anybody to join our protest. Indeed, we felt a kind of perverse satisfaction in seeing Rick's stuff, which had been totally excluded from the original dummy, replace ours.

By the way, the book quickly became a success; one of Straight Arrow's few good sellers. It is even being reissued today by another publisher, and no doubt Mr. Estren has already received his check. But to the best of my knowledge, no artist other than Crumb has ever been paid a penny for *A History of Underground Comics*. I'd like to be proved wrong on that.

Underground Cartoonist: Zippy the Pinhead, Arcade, Young Lust

Late 1970 or 1971: My first meeting with Robert. It was in Art Spiegelman's room in a run-down residential hotel on Sixteenth Street in San Francisco. I offered my hand in greeting but Crumb refused it, saying he didn't do "the hippie handshake." Actually, neither did I and it was an awkward moment. Later, he said he liked *Young Lust*, my first underground success. I breathed a sigh of relief. I remember my image of him from his work was one of an old guy, possibly Jewish, and very touchy. Well, one out of three isn't bad.

Nineteen seventy-three: Potter Valley, California. Robert and Aline's "shack" next to Dana's house. I noticed the refrigerator was completely filled with Coca-Cola. Robert and Dana's then-little son, Jesse, referred to Aline as "Smearface Bonbon" and, when I went for a walk with him along the Eel River, kicked me in the shins.

Nineteen seventy-six or 1977: Diane and I are house-sitting for Robert and Aline. On our visits to their place in Madison,

135

California, I always enjoyed looking at Robert's collection of old stuff: toy cars, joke placards, unopened jars, boxes and bottles of pomade, tooth powder, soft drinks, and headache remedies, all with beautifully designed labels and logos, mostly from the twenties and thirties (things now hoarded and overpriced as "kitsch collectibles"). But the night we stayed alone in the cluttered (neatly cluttered) house, I couldn't sleep, tossing and turning as a sense of claustrophobia grew in on me. All the bulging display cases and crowded shelves seemed too much, pushing the air out of the room. Without Robert and Aline there, amid the stuff, the "context" was removed and I felt overwhelmed.

Nineteen seventy-eight or 1979: Showing Robert one of my *Griffith Observatory* strips titled "The Cuteness Syndrome." This was my attempt to demonstrate how "reality" is deviously transformed into "cuteness" by a process of infantilization. Making the head bigger in proportion to the body, eyes bigger and further apart, et cetera. Crumb read the page and then said, "Bill, these 'cute' drawings aren't cute. You just can't do 'cute'!" I laughed uneasily.

Nineteen eighty-five or 1986: Walking the hot, dry hills around Robert's house in Winters, California. The kind of "timeless" isolation that attracted Robert to this backwater region was beginning to change. Big, ugly modern houses were going up around Crumb's humble cottage. These encroaching commuters from Sacramento always built their "Ponderosas" on the tops of hills and, as a result, Robert said, through some acoustical quirk, he could actually hear the yahoos arguing all the way from his front porch. I pointed out that the encroachers could probably also hear Robert and Aline from their houses. Robert said, "That's right! Why, those dirty…," and kicked a clod of dirt in disgust.

Nineteen ninety: Diane and I are sharing a cabin with Robert, Aline, and Sophie at Lake Tahoe. One day we dragged Robert away from his huge jigsaw puzzle and paid a visit to the casinos just over the state line in Nevada. While

Diane hit the slots, arranging to meet Aline and Sophie later in the hotel pool, Crumb and I prowled the casino floor, muttering and complaining about Modern America. "Harrah's Club" seemed to epitomize all the hopeless striving and know-nothing materialism of our fellow citizens and we reveled in our alienation and snot-nosed superiority. When we rejoined Diane, she told us she'd just hit three hundred dollars on a dollar machine and showed us her winnings (and complimentary coffee mug). I was happy to see the gleaming coins, but Robert called it "ill-gotten gains" and said we had to spend it all immediately on a fancy dinner at the most expensive restaurant in the joint.

Nineteen ninety-two: Visiting the Crumbs in their medieval fortress in southern France. Robert's tentative attempt at learning the French language consisted of weekly viewings of the *French in Action* TV series, a course which focused on the daily life of Mireille—a terminally perky, self-absorbed young Frenchwoman. Crumb's British neighbor, Nick, would come by to ease the pain. I joined them one day in what amounted to a lesson in French-language work avoidance. Within a few minutes of "Leçon 12," the proceedings degenerated into comments on Mireille's anatomical endowments and pouty lips. At one point, when Mireille is shown running across a plaza to catch a bus, Robert pushed the "slow" button on the remote to more carefully observe her "French in action." "Ooh la la !" he murmured. End of Leçon 12.

Nineteen ninety-six: Robert and I talking comics (his and mine) at a party in Dixon, California. "Your stuff," he said, referring to my daily *Zippy* strip, "is really great, but I have one criticism." I braced myself. "You've got to make Zippy and Zerbina's kids look more kidlike," he said. "It's hard to tell them apart from their parents." I promised I'd work on it.

Later in 1996: Crumb and I are in my newly installed hot tub in my backyard in San Francisco. After an initial resistance Robert tested the bubbling waters and settled in for a soak. After a few minutes discussing our various cartooning-related aches and pains, we both began recounting our brushes with "Hollywood" and the nightmarish dealings with lawyers, producers, and agents they brought up. At one point I complained about a "net-profit participation" clause in a particularly obnoxious contract being offered to me. Robert said, "Net??? Bubby, 'net' is for fish! Go for gross points, bubby!" I was struck by the fact that we were actually discussing show biz in a hot tub in California and mentioned this to Crumb. We let the irony just wash over us.

Nineteen ninety-seven: I take Robert to an out-of-the-way restaurant I think he'll like. It's called the Tennessee Grille, located in the Outer Sunset, an aggressively unhip San Francisco neighborhood. The house specials are distinctly all-American. Robert orders the pot roast, I go for the Southern fried chicken. When his meal is served, Crumb almost mists over, fork poised. He stares tenderly at his steaming plate, piled high with slices of beef, mounds of homemade mashed potatoes, and a "vegetable medley." After a long pause Robert says, "Beautiful. You just don't see this kind of thing in France." I respond, "It's a lovely still life," and we both dig in.

G E O R G E   P A U L U S

Record Producer: The Pretty Things, Big Mojo, El Dorados

I took a drag from my glowing square and placed it in its temporary resting place in the cheap, dented tin ashtray. As my hand reached for the beer nestled on the coffee table, I mused about the decor of the 10' x 12' living room. The ashtray was encrusted with years of trace ash that never really got washed off. This ashtray didn't take baths and none were administered to it.

The aptly named coffee table was stained by spilled coffee to the point that the factory varnish paled in comparison to the nutty sienna luster provided by the extract of the little brown beans. Stacks of magazines rested on the geriatric table with only pencils and the odd fork as accents to the apartment decor.

Looking left and right in the garden apartment, my eyes focused on the ever increasing rows of reel-to-reel tapes huddled in the cheapest of metal shelves. Like little musical high-rise projects, the shelves were filled to the bursting point and constantly growing.

Smoky, dirt-sodden white paint did its best to clothe the cracked plaster walls. Three generic light fixtures that simply held the bulbs were fore, aft, and above. A floor that had not had the benefit of a rug to protect it from decades of foot traffic just lay there.

The unsprung couch offered a good vantage point from which to watch the roaches. A few glistening brown shells would appear with the creatures' little feelers twirling in the close air. Small platoons would make their almost mindless forays across the ground, looking for nonexistent food. You could stamp your feet and the insect scouts would depart for a few moments and quickly return en masse with their urban brethren. At times, it was actually fascinating to view them poking their wiggling little heads out of magazine pages, scurrying behind record stacks, climbing out of a coffee cup, or resting between the folds of a towel. This was the urban ecosystem in all its earthy writhing glory. Marty accepted these little squatters in a truly pacifist manner.

"Ready for another beer?" asked Marty Pahls. "Yep," I casually replied. Marty entered the room and placed the brew in a small area curiously left vacant between the magazine mountain ranges. As I reached for another square and fired it up, Marty's pale white hand deftly darted into my pack of smokes, extracting one for himself.

Marty and I traded music tapes on a regular basis, and discussed music and art at every opportunity. This was the point in time that hip blues record collectors were discovering Robert Johnson, Charlie Patton, and scores of unknown players on vintage shellac. The items were traded among collectors, or taped, so at least one could hear these rare little beasts. Marty forced me to listen to twenties jazz and hillbilly. I forced him to listen to postwar blues and ducktail rockabilly. Even cultural exchange.

It was 1969. I had just made twenty-one. Marty was a handful of years older. We had met at the Jazz Record Mart on the Near North Side of Chicago. I was selling some spare blues 78s to the cheap bearded owner of the store.

"Are you into blues?" a voice queried. I turned slowly and viewed a male figure dressed in garments with no discernible style. A rumpled coat, a cheap scarf, plain shirt and pants, and generic beat-up black shoes clothed this guy with a crazy grin on his face. He probably experienced culture shock as he viewed me in shoulder length hair, leather coat, and South Side manners.

Marty and I became fast, close friends. He turned me on to R. Crumb in an in-depth way in very short order. Crumb and Pahls were ancient friends. Marty had married Crumb's sister. Robert gave Marty one of his bursting sketchbooks. It was one of Marty's treasured possessions. The whole Crumb lexicon was right there in ink—a crash course in Crumb 101 and 102. His work knocked me out. It was like learning a new language. I was hooked like a trout on a stainless-steel barb.

At our weekly musical get-together, Marty mentioned that Crumb was coming to Chicago the next week. I asked if Robert might possibly do a drawing for my struggling blues record label. Marty responded that Crumb was more likely to do some artwork for me than for some big corporate concern. Marty smiled knowingly and added, "You might offer him some of your prewar blues or jazz 78s in trade for some artwork." When I got home, I assembled about twenty-five shellac 78s spares for Robert to check out.

I arrived early at Marty's dump the evening of "Crumb arrival day." No effort had been made to tidy up the joint. My tin ashtray was in its usual resting place and a beer was in my hand within moments. Marty announced that a couple of Chicago "artists" would also be joining us. I cringed. Marty laughed and cautioned me not to be too tough on the North Siders. No one came close to Crumb.

The local artists arrived without any fanfare; even the insects were nonplussed. One short, thin couple had that laid-back ambience with the underlying North Side upper-crust feel. Birkenstock, before Birkenstock was even invented. They did bring good weed, though. As the numbers were fired up, the doorbell rang. Shudders amongst the faithful. False alarm. It was only the other local artist couple. They were larger in size and importance.

Small talk, really small talk, about their little comic denizens. I got another beer and sank back into my soft chair and got progressively more stoned. It was the only defense against the bullshit. They used words in the same way they used pens. Endlessly modeling their turds till they fooled other folks into not believing they were still looking at—turds.

As Crumb's arrival drew closer, the artists became more animated, their conversations more feigned. They nervously scratched their arms and faux afros. The women's hands turned into combs to rearrange their hair. Their breasts became more perky as their backs arched. Eyes searched for something besides the roaches. The messiah would soon be here.

The doorbell screeched out its shrill disjointed tone. Marty got up and heaved the heavy door open. In shuffled Robert Crumb, looking more like a scuffling thirties dance band musician than an underground artist. Marty greeted his old friend as old friends will do. "Hi, Robert," Marty beamed with genuine friendliness. Crumb almost stumbled through the narrow hallway and quietly made his way to the living room. He took off his fedora and coat and looked for a place to deposit them.

Crumb stood there with his usual forlorn stance. In spite of his obvious vulnerability, Bob looked almost ready for the onslaught of the locals. The North Siders engaged him with talk of God knows what. I tried not to listen. The artist couples were circling Crumb. Maybe they thought their "art" would improve as they breathed the same dank air. Marty was the only person in the room who didn't grab for a piece of Crumb. I grabbed another beer and waited my turn to talk to the master.

As Robert defensively surveyed the apartment in between comic talk, he noticed a pile of 78s on the table. Crumb simply stopped talking and walked away from the group to the shellac stack. "Marty, where'd you get these?"

Crumb queried with delight. Marty answered that they were George's records.

Quick introductions having been made, Robert and I engaged in deep talk about prewar black bluesmen and hillbilly artists. The comic artists looked at us strangely. What the hell was I talking about that had gotten Crumb's rapt attention? I quickly told Robert that I loved his art. The records were brought along with the thought of trading records for artwork. Marty mentioned I had recorded a down-home blues harp player and his band from Chicago's Maxwell Street. "The real thing," Marty added. "I have thousands of seventy-eights," I chimed in. Crumb sheepishly asked when I wanted to get together.

Crumb and I made the forty-five-minute drive from the North to the South Side talking mostly about music. As we passed the projects, we tossed the fantasies back and forth about how many great old unfound records might remain in the broken-down houses and concrete bunkers. The records were still around; it just took real digging to find them. These neighborhoods could be dangerous, but the music was even more dangerous. We stopped at a few junk shops on the Far South Side and Crumb did find a really hot hillbilly record by Lester Smallwood. A good start for a day that would bring forth some killer artwork.

We arrived at my mother's bungalow and upon reaching the basement where I reigned, Crumb politely asked if he could look at the 78s. "Wow!" he said. "It's great to have the basement to yourself, surrounded by all these neat records." After pawing through rows of vintage 78s, Crumb shyly noted that the records he had amassed were really great. "Fine," I said. "They're yours." Robert laughed and said how strange it was to get these really rare jazz records just for some drawings. "Great art for great art," I said. "It seems pretty fair to me."

"Do you have some paper and pens?" he inquired. I brought forth some ordinary-grade paper and a selection of pens. "Sorry, Bob, I don't use rapido-graph pens much. I paint in oils." Crumb asked what I wanted him to do.

143

I described the area on Maxwell Street where the musicians played and put on the record I had recorded in my very basement. "These guys sound pretty good. I didn't think stuff like this was still being played," Crumb said excitedly. "There's still a bunch of real blues players around at little black South and West Side clubs," I explained. Since I didn't have pictures of them, Robert asked that I describe the band and their attire. I ended up posing, hunched up with a microphone, assuming the position of the blues cats on Maxwell Street. Robert asked that I be the judge as to whether the drawing was any good. The usual Crumb self-effacing nature, hoping the drawing is okay. He respected musicians and took special care in their portrayal.

Robert started drawing the "band" leader of the blues trio first. "Just correct me if I'm doing something wrong," he said as he put lines on paper that breathed the persona of the musicians. From the little folds in the sport coat to the jaunty fedora to the uplifting process on the guitar player, the paper came to life, magically, in a couple of hours in between talking and looking at vintage 78s. When it was finished, Robert even laughed that nervous laugh and ventured that it looked pretty good. "Fucking great," I intoned. "It's absolutely perfect." "Maybe it'll help you sell some records; it's really good that you're recording these guys before they die," he said.

On the ride back to Marty's place, Crumb and I talked more music and about further trades of records for art. He went through the reasons why a big ass was an important quality in a female, how hippie music basically sucked, and how the hippie philosophy was bullshit. "Fuck *Playboy*!" Crumb shouted. "I'd only do a drawing for them if they let me do the cover!"

Crumb was genuine, friendly, and weirdly funny, and shuffled along like a struggling dance band musician who would rather be playing jazz on the black South Side of Chicago, watching those big-ass women shake their shimmy, than do some expensive uptown gig playin' waltzes.

As you can see, Bob, the experience was "tight like that."

Illustrator/Cartoonist: Wired, Time, Mondo 2000, Heavy Metal

Who can forget their first exposure to *Zap Comix*? Mine occurred during 1968 in the Sinaloa Junior High School Library. Someone in our "gang" had brought *Zap* #3 (the dual Griffin/Wilson covered one) to school, and let me tell you, it was a *big* hit. People were frantically jockeying for a chance to read it. I was fortunate enough to have an entire "study" period in the library to peruse this masterpiece, only having to share it with two other people. We managed to sit quietly and read it without attracting the head librarian's attention. To this day, I doubt she would have appreciated the literary merits of S. Clay Wilson's Captain Pissgums....

I was amazed to find that comics, something that an interest in would have brought scorn and derison only a year or two earlier, were now "cool." Soon there were lots of places to buy this new type of "comix." Even our little hick town had a "head shop," and there were literally tons of comix, a veritable avalanche of the stuff. But the best comix were always by Crumb. Seeing a Crumb cover or finding a Crumb story in a book was a guarantee that it was well worth buying. He had it all: amusing stories, hilarious characters, inventive concepts, a healthy disrespect of authority, and great art. Did I say great art? I meant *great* art!!! This guy could really draw. His style was aped by every up-and-coming artist in the country. If you were to get a phone book from the early seventies and look in the yellow pages at the ads, you'd find nothing but imitations of Robert's take on big-foot cartooning and old-fashioned lettering, with lots of the obligatory rapidograph line work.

Yet Crumb proved to be more than a flash in the pan. He continued to improve, producing even better work year after year. If it's an artist's job to build his own "monument" by the quality and quantity of the work he produces, then R. Crumb has built one hell of a monument.

Years later I actually had a chance to talk to the "great man" himself. I was in the process of trying to put together my own comix anthology, *Buzz*, and had sent letters of solicitation to many talented artists, including Crumb. I figured it couldn't hurt to hope for the best.

Naturally, I didn't hear back from him. As a matter of fact, at that point in time I was seriously concerned if I'd be able to gather enough quality material to even do the book. It was in this pessimistic state that I received a phone call one afternoon. "Hi. This is Robert Crumb," the voice said. Unfortunately, the voice sounded exactly like my brother-in-law's, and I was sure he was toying with me. I was considering what would be the cleverest way to tell him to go screw himself when I realized the voice was a little different....

It was R. Crumb and fortunately I didn't insult him. Robert was in the process of folding *Weirdo*, and was kind enough to help out with recommendations, addresses, and a boxload of great, unused submissions.

So, twenty years after I was flabbergasted by those great R. Crumb comics, I enjoyed a pleasant afternoon conversation with the artist himself.

146

Underground Cartoonist: The Adventures of Jesus, Feelgood Funnies

In July 1968 Gilbert Shelton wrote to me from California (the first I'd heard from him in about a year): "I'm publishing a little comic book myself for underground distribution in the psychedelic shops across the country and should be through printing in about a week. It's called *Feds 'n' Heads* ... I'll send you a copy since you might otherwise never see one in Columbia. (Or am I mistaken in my assumption about the Missouri scene?) If somebody had told me five years ago how many heads and reds and radicals there would be in Austin in 1968, I wouldn't have believed them...."

On November 14 (about two weeks after Richard Nixon had been elected president), he wrote: "I've decided to stay out in San Francisco for a while ... I've met a bunch of cartoonists out here, and there's an active scene going on. I'm sending *Zap Comix* #s 1 and 2 as examples. Robert Crumb's address is: 705 Clayton, San Francisco. There's another comic book like this, just out, called *Bijou Funnies*;

for a copy of that write Jay Lynch, 1757 N. Mohawk, Chicago.... Also, although harder to find, *Snatch Comics* by R. Crumb and S. Clay Wilson—a total assault on porn and smut (under the counter, 50 cents/$1.00)."

But Gilbert wasn't exactly right about the Missouri scene. People were already bringing *Zaps* back from California, and there were some underground publications available—under the counter—at head shops and some newsstands. The University of Missouri had its own Vietnam War protests with panicky officials calling out the National Guard.

The revelation of *Feds 'n' Heads* (featuring those Fabulous Furry Freak Brothers), *Snatch,* and *Zap* was that anyone could publish anything they could draw. As Robert Crumb was reported to have said, "Before I'd been censoring *myself!*" But the elation I felt on seeing Crumb's and S. Clay Wilson's cartoons in *Zap* was a lot more than a sense of possibilities opening up. The possibilities were realized already. Their stuff was so good! As Gilbert described Crumb in a postcard to me: "He's a real genius, not a phony one."

The pages of *Zap* were wildly and ferociously funny, uncompromising, unsentimental, defiant. They were about our lives and our world. Whiteman, Flakey Foont, Mr. Natural, and the Old Pooperoo became instant mythology. Was Flakey Foont Crumb himself? You might have thought so if Crumb had not introduced himself on the inside front cover of the first two issues as an absurd, idealistic, angry neurotic and, as he characterized himself subsequently, a sex-obsessed intellectual. He becomes a great comic himself in the character of that incorrigible reprobate, R. Crumb. Here we were introduced to a great creative talent on his own turf, already at his full strength, defining the fantastic serious possibilities of a hitherto despised medium—his medium—THE COMIC BOOK.

The other artists in the early *Zaps* proved that great possibilities were really there for other artists. With his comic strip *The Freak Brothers*, Shelton finally asserted his great comic flair—evident for years, but finally working easily and gracefully with his deep intelligence and talent as a storyteller. Victor Moscoso's work was not really very funny. It was mysterious and surrealistic—a true heir of Winsor McCay's *Little Nemo*. For immediate impact, S. Clay Wilson's outrageous pirates and bikers were the most challenging feature of the book. They were unforgivably, intransigently offensive. His overcrowded panels, reminiscent of classic zany strips like Bill Holman's *Smokey Stover* and Will Elder's *Mad* comic book parodies, were beautifully composed. The supernaturally impossible adventures were accompanied by disarming, unself-conscious dialogue and an elegant mock-heroic narrative. With the addition of Rick Griffin, Spain, and Robert Williams, *Zap* became the focus of the underground "movement." Suddenly it seemed there was an abundance of talent in the country, just waiting for an opportunity to show what they could do.

Seemed? It was true. Remarkable talents did appear and blossom in the underground comic books during the next few years; some only briefly, but others as permanent fixtures: Skip Williamson, Trina Robbins, Bill Griffith, Jay Lynch, Greg Irons, Kim Deitch, Justin Green, and Ted Richards. The boom didn't really last very long—only three or four years, until the great newsprint shortage of 1973.

As for the effect that *Zap* had on me, it was like a rush of adrenaline—a deep psychic, almost erotic thrill. Gilbert and the Texas Crowd, including Fred Todd and Dave Moriaty, set up the Rip Off Press, and my *New Adventures of Jesus* was one of their first projects. It came out in November 1969, and after that I drew four more books just as fast as I could: *Jesus Meets the Armed Services*, in 1970; *Feelgood Funnies*, in 1971; and *Amazon* and *Jesus Joins the Academic Community*, in 1972. Gilbert Shelton and Rip Off Press are directly responsible for all those comic strips of mine being created as well as being published. There was even a little bit of money in it, though not very much. The great thing about working for Rip Off was that they published everything that I sent them, and they never asked me to change anything. They took the economic chances, the public outrage, and the critical lumps. Rip Off Press, the Print Mint, Last Gasp, and publishers like Gary Arlington, Denis Kitchen, and Jay Lynch, among others, struggled to keep the underground alive for the artists as long as they could. They never got petty or greedy. It seemed that everyone understood the value of encouraging all the artists to do their own thing.

Crumb and Shelton were then, and still are, the center of it all. Just seeing their work always made me want to dip my pen and start drawing. The underground may seem moribund today, but that's essentially because the old economics have changed, and the avenues of head shop distribution have basically closed down. Robert Crumb is as good as and as active as ever. Shelton lives in Paris, where he is a major celebrity, publishing his work in various European comic magazines and also in this country.

In my opinion, Crumb is the best comic book artist who ever lived—and Shelton is his best competition. The first several issues of *Zap*, even as "lowly comic books," compete with the best art and literature of the last couple decades. Crumb and Shelton are national treasures alongside James Thurber, Rockwell Kent, John Ford, and Elzie Segar.

R A L P H   S T E A D M A N

Illustrator: Fear and Loathing in Las Vegas, Alice in Wonderland

I am happy to say that R. Crumb has never influenced me in the slightest. His greatest contribution to humanity is Mr. Natural and his style is just weirdly his own. If he has any imitators, then they should be restrained. His kind of art should only happen once.

I think I have met him about twice and on both occasions he has reminded me of someone who has forgotten to bring his greasy gabardine raincoat. He also kept his hat on, so he is probably as bald as his most famous character and quite without a grain of common courtesy for another. I doubt we have two words in common and if we have, then they are probably "Piss off." That does not in any way denote a disregard for each other. On the contrary, it probably suggests a mutual recognition of each other's art, as one neighborhood dog to another who marks out his particular territory and hunkers down. Apart from that, I doubt if there is anything else I can add, except good luck for the next twenty years, R. Crumb.

S . C L A Y W I L S O N

Underground Cartoonist: Zap, The Checkered Demon

The first time I saw Crumb's work was a comic strip entitled *Stoned* in *Cavalier* magazine that somebody handed me at a party in Lawrence, Kansas, in 1967. I really dug it. I was dropping lots of acid and working on a portfolio of twenty drawings to be published by Charles Plymell.

Plymell: poet, novelist, beat character, and collage artist from Wichita, Kansas, was guest artist for *Grist*, a local poetry-prose-art magazine. He liked my work and asked me to be a contributor to future issues. I was flattered and glad to do so. Later, Charlie offered to do this limited edition Twenty Drawings portfolio (the original price was four dollars and now they're collector's items selling for three thousand dollars). I was working on this project when Plymell split to San Francisco.

In February of 1968 a bunch of us decided to make our get-away from the Midwest and headed for "the cool gray city of love"

153

in a Volkswagen bus. Among my earthly possessions was a box of the now completed portfolios, one of which I was going to lay on Plymell when I looked him up in Frisco.

When I visited Charlie, he was busy printing the first *Zap* comic as I handed him a portfolio, which he hadn't seen yet, and he dug it. At this time I met Don Donahue, who was there to buy Plymell's press—the genesis of Apex Novelties, Donahue's publishing/printing company for "future" underground comix. This first *Zap* was done entirely by Crumb featuring a two-color cover (blue and orange) and is now another collector's item (if it says "Printed by Charles Plymell" in small blue type on the back cover).

Donahue liked my portfolio and offered to introduce me to Crumb. This sounded okay to me since I had seen Crumb's work, liked it, and wanted to give him a portfolio (which he later chopped up).

When I met Crumb we talked, smoked some pot, and drew some cartoons. At this point Crumb invited me to do some comic strips for *Zap Comix* #2, since he wanted to do a larger issue featuring other artists working in a "similar vein." Victor Moscoso and Rick Griffin then contributed since they were using comic strip images in the rock posters they were doing with a psychedelic twist. Later, I talked Crumb (a repressed Catholic choirboy) into drawing "dirty..." that is drawing *anything* that occurred to him, without censorship or concern for an imagined audience. He took my advice and did so with relish. This all seems like it happened yesterday.

Painter/Composer: Hackett Freedman Gallery, El Mariachi

"The exhilarating thing about shock is the aristocratic pleasure of giving offense."—Charles Baudelaire

Robert Crumb has a secure spot in the canon of comics. He has carved out a territory that is his own. His work, like heavy metal and rap music, is unparodyable.

My parents had a copy of *Zap* #0 on a shelf by the tools near the back of our house, when I was five or six. It had the same air as a lot of things that were of the world of adults, like the whiskey my uncle poured into his Coke in the movie theater when he took me to see *Willy Wonka and the Chocolate Factory*. This "adult air" was the initial lure to investigate the comic further. I would look at the cover (with the guy's butt plugged in) and then I'd read through some of the insides, curious but urged on because I knew I wasn't quite supposed to be looking at it, and that was it.

Between then and now, I have occasionally picked up something of his. Either I'd be curious about his work once again, or people whose opinions I respected would comment about how good he really was. I'd be flipping through it and the drawings would always bait me, so I'd bring it home to have a closer look. I'd start out looking at, and reading, every word, but his excessive use of exclamatory sentences (and drawings) were so similar that I found myself skimming over the work and stopping only occasionally to check on story movement or when a drawing *really* grabbed me.

With Crumb, the drawing is the lure. Those little lines, the dots and wobbles, the character, weight, balance, and meatiness of his panels and illustrations give his work that unwashed look—the little details that come from looking all the time. Some of his drawings pull me into them, most always his black-and-white ones. Crumb's color doesn't live up to his line work. It just sits on top of the drawing, like part of a separate, less interesting conversation. The color doesn't integrate with the drawing, tonally. This is much like the way black-and-white movies were "colorized," when colorization first came into practice. Its existing structure did not need flat panes of color over it. Finally, the taboo quality of Crumb's work kept up too loud of a drumbeat and drowned out the finer, more discreet instruments. This repeated low sharp note, recognizable on the second beat, was what I always found tiresome and disappointing. It's why I'd seldom finish one of his stories. I'd close the cover and put it back down.

Underground Cartoonist: Binky Brown Meets the Holy Virgin Mary

Zap #0 and #1 are like *Mad* prior to #28, before Gaines took the reins from Kurtzman. Just as the ten-cent *Mad* color comic created the notoriety that the larger format magazine was to enjoy, it was the all-Crumb issues of *Zap* that kicked off the momentum which the later *Zap* anthologies were to capitalize on. In fact, it was Crumb's work which was the seminal influence on the whole underground cartooning phenomenon.

Back in the late sixties, most cartoonists in the movement were rank beginners learning in public. Regardless of stylistic quirks, these amateurs (like myself) were able to get published and circulated because of the booming "alternate culture." I never bought the idea that we were part of a subculture separated from the mainstream. I thought of the real terrain of the underground as being "the edge" of personal imperative to realize a vision or to make a statement. Thirty years later, most of us that are still

157

cartooning have stepped a few paces back from that edge. More than a hand-ful are gone forever—if not directly because of the occupation itself, then because of the lifestyle that living and working at such an intensity too often demands.

Luckily for *Zap*, its name got to be a generic term for the movement it spearheaded. To the uninitiated, all titles were called "Zap" comics. The *Zap* artists became the established orthodoxy of renegade cartooning. Within a very diverse field of talent, they commanded an elite niche. In other words, they got a lot more than the going page rate. They were a little bit older than the rest of the cartoonists, too. In terms of artistic skill and business savvy, the gap of a few years was critical.

In the future, any historian wanting to do a glossing over of the heyday of underground comix will have a ready-made leitmotif in the word *Zap*. As the years go by, that repeated emphasis on *Zap* will overshadow the dozens of other titles that can legitimately claim to be first-rate.

R I C H A R D   S A L A

Illustrator/Cartoonist: MTV's Liquid Television, Raw, Esquire, Playboy

Like a lot of cartoonists, I drew and stapled together my own comics when I was a kid. Probably my biggest influence was (and still is!) Chester Gould. I wasn't that interested in superheroes though, so as I entered my teen years, I was spending less time at the comics racks and more time hanging out in record stores and libraries. Being a typically confused, angry, depressed teenager, my reading tastes leaned toward the bleak, the existential, and the nihilistic. It was around then—the early seventies—that I stumbled upon underground comics. They seemed sort of depraved until I realized they were right up my alley: they were bleak, existential, and nihilistic, plus they were really funny!

I had seen R. Crumb's drawings before on some "funny valentine" gum cards and in fanzines, and his style was instantly recognizable—the logos, the cars, the gurls! I kept *Carload o' Comics* and a digest-sized Fritz the Cat book hidden in a dresser drawer.

This was because, although my mom had been pretty tolerant about all the comics and monster magazines cluttering up my room, I simply didn't think she'd understand that I found Crumb's portrayal of his sexual obsessions funny and liberating, rather than—as my mom would surely see it—sick. Plus, underground comix were practically synonymous with drug use, and I didn't dare read them openly, lest my mom forbid me to hang out at the teen center dances, or worse, throw out my comics!

My favorite Crumb stories were the hilariously "autobiographical" ones, like "The Confessions of R. Crumb," "The Many Faces of R. Crumb," "R. Crumb Versus the Sisterhood," "The R. Crumb ucke$$ Story," et cetera. I really liked the idea of an artist putting himself in his stories, giving an element of *truth* to absurd tales and fantasies. *Artistic Comics* was another revelation: printing pages from Crumb's sketchbooks seemed to confirm that undergrounds were indeed something more than trashy hippie sex rags. Those sketchbook pages were alive with the *joy* of drawing.

I began drawing again myself, filling up notebooks with obsessively detailed pictures and cryptic, bitter poetry. Eventually, I went to art school and, in the early eighties, there were new and exciting developments: *Raw*, Mark Beyer's wonderful *Dead Stories* and, lo and behold, Crumb's *Weirdo*—among the best work he'd ever done! This was all very inspiring and, before I knew it, I was drawing my *own* comics!

Cartoonist/Illustrator: Garbage Pail Kids

I would like to say that upon first exposure to Robert Crumb's cartoons, my trembling adolescent personality was instantly shattered, my ego and worldly ambitions melted away, and a brilliant white light clearly revealed in ten thousand rushing mutating visions the path that lay before me as an artist; my mission in life, which would require me to plumb the absolute depths of my soul—unflinchingly facing unbearable pain, ecstasy, hatred, laughter, and fear—and express as fully as humanly possible in deeply penetrating comix and paintings the profound, paradoxical truths of life, to enlighten and entertain my fellow humans, and so, despite obstacles and doubts … No! No! That's *all bullshit*. But that's how it should have gone, right? Actually, I was *already* doing cartooning in high school in 1968 when I discovered *R. Crumb's Head Comix* and *Zap* at a local head shop one day after school.

Crumb's art was clear and confident. He's an artist who had

found and developed his own voice at a young age. Part of his art's visual appeal, I learned, came from his early work in greeting cards. Even his ugliest stuff had a cute, friendly edge, and vice versa. Everything he drew became a full, living, breathing, familiar presence. Other comic books, particularly superheroes, seemed pale, mechanical, and cold next to his work … less human, even. But Crumb's images just seemed to ooze their way into my brain.

While there were many aspects of his work I enjoyed, and continue to enjoy, it was Crumb's fluency and directness of expression that I most liked. His art radiated a raw passion for cartoon imagery, and seeing it gave me hope that the art process would not always be sheer drudgery; and that I *too* could somehow tap into the universal lightning rod, or whatever it is, that dwells within.

Little did I know that years later, after stumbling through various grueling comix and illustration projects, I would find a similar fluency and directness in my own work, in creating hundreds of *Garbage Pail Kids* stickers for Topps (a company that had also hired Crumb and many other underground cartoonists for projects). Working with Art Spiegelman and Mark Newgarden on the series was a gas! Although there was a huge amount of work involved, the paintings and ideas just poured out, with no obstacles. I felt like I'd hit a very fertile vein of creative weirdness, with that same "plugged-in" feeling promised on the cover of *Zap* #0.

J A Y   K I N N E Y

Cartoonist/Editor: Anarchy Comics, Young Lust, Occult Laff-Parade

The further the sixties and seventies recede behind clichéd myths promulgated by the media and our own nostalgia, the harder it becomes to pinpoint the significant impact that Robert Crumb has had. Much of that impact was indirect and covert, which is not surprising since Crumb seemed to like it that way.

In my own case, I doubt that I would have become as involved with underground comix as I did if not for Crumb's inspiring role as bashful smart aleck. Although Crumb's *Zap* #1 was not the first underground comic, *Zap* was the comic that excited other cartoonists to push their own limits and go for broke.

Go for broke is probably an apt phase because no small part of Crumb's charisma was his resolute anticommercialism. For better or for worse, his hatred of "sharpies" and hip capitalists helped shape other artists' suspicions of success into an antisellout ideology which both preserved the comix' purity for far longer than one would have expected and cinched their marginal economic status. Had any other cartoonist created Fritz the Cat, Mr. Natural, or Flakey Foont, he would be a millionaire today and we would be awash in Fritz dolls, Mr. Natural paperbacks, and Foont pillowcases. But Crumb resisted the temptation.

He also pioneered the use of the comics medium as a personal confessional, where the artist bares all for his unseen audience. Justin Green's *Binky Brown Meets the Holy Virgin Mary* and Art Spiegelman's *Maus* may represent the most fully realized instances of such soul bearing, but year in, year out, no one has been more honest (and ironically amusing) about his neuroses and eccentricities than Crumb—with the possible exception of his wife, Aline!

Last but not least, Crumb set the standard for draftsmanship in comix, and I am hard pressed to name anyone who has topped him in fluid line work or range of styles. Crumb made drawing look easy and fun—an illusion which sustained me for a number of years before I decided it was actually a labor intensive grind. But Crumb draws on, as effortlessly and beautifully as ever.

Of course, no genius is perfect, and Crumb has, at times, been his own worst enemy. As a magazine publisher, I would hesitate to give him a cover assignment unless I was prepared to accept a design from him which seemed guaranteed to kill newsstand sales. Art which springs from his own enthusiasms and motivations can be exquisite, but catch him in a contrary mood (or make him an offer that he can't refuse) and Lord knows what you'll get. Crumb is fully capable of taking the worst stereotypes and pushing them to such an extreme that they implode into ridiculousness. However, that can be a joke that not everyone gets and it has earned him his fair share of censure over the years.

Nevertheless, when all is said and done, I consider Crumb to be one of few true originals in the field. Both underground and alternative comics owe him an enormous debt, and on a personal note, he remains a creative mentor to me now nearly thirty years since we first met. I just hope that the art supply companies continue to make pen nibs and india ink for as long as he lives.

M A R Y   F L E E N E R

Cartoonist: Weirdo, Slutburger, Twisted Sisters, Life of the Party

You can say a lot of things both pro and con about Robert Crumb, but no one can deny that reading his pages in *Zap Comix* for the first time dramatically changed everyone's definition of cartooning, especially mine. In fact, Crumb is responsible for making me the liberated woman I am today. Not only was I inspired artistically by his work, but it was his articulation of social satire that helped release a part of my personality that I'd been struggling to suppress because other people told me it wasn't "ladylike" or "mature." (That *little* demon in me that laughed too loud and at the wrong times, that questioned authority and asked "why?") Crumb's work reinforced my bad attitude and for that I'm forever grateful.

Along with thousands of other kids, I studied and tried to copy the "look" of Crumb. We doodled Mr. Naturals on our notebooks and painted Keep On Truckin' on everything else. Yes, *Zap* was even used for rolling joints, but I never considered underground comix part of the "drug culture"—they were more than that. Crumb and his fellow artists started an art movement on the streets of America, not in some High Temple of Gallery Elitism that catered to the economic playground of investors and so-called royalty. The underground comix criticized society and had something to say. They were interesting and provocative—something that had been missing in the art world for a long time.

The first day I saw these comics in 1969, I knew right then that someday I would be creating similar stuff, but I waited a *considerable* amount of time to actually sit down and work. What really got me going was an article that Matt Groening had written for the *L.A. Reader* in 1984. It was about the "new style" of underground comix and it contained Robert Crumb's address. He was, literally, the first person that I ever wrote to and I sent him my first attempts.

My character was "Li'l Mofo," a black flea that lived on a white dog and spoke in an exaggerated Afro-American dialect, which I guess could be considered "racist" by knee-jerk definition. But I knew Crumb would get it since he drew Angelfood McSpade. What a surprise it was to receive a reply and a copy of *Weirdo*. He was very encouraging. I couldn't believe it! One of my neighbors was watering his lawn and I came running over, going, "Look! Look at this *great* comic! This is the new *Weirdo*! The editor wrote me! R. Crumb! Isn't that great?" To which he replied, "Yeah! Great! Who's R. Crumb?"and thus I learned my first lesson in being an underground cartoonist.

I knew Crumb had a reputation as a flirt, so I wasn't too surprised when he started adding comments like,"Send me your picture." So I decided to mess with him a little bit. I drew a "Day in the Life" comic strip for him with pictures of *my* face pasted on Frederick's of Hollywood girly drawings. I had all the sexy bodies washing dishes, exercising, drawing, and I even included an S/M couple on the last panel and explained that this was how my husband and I relaxed at the end of the day. Crumb's reply did not disappoint—he said he was going to "squeeze my face" and "pound my butt" because I was such a

"Smart Ass." He also gave me plenty of good advice, like "Draw it the way you want it to look," and most importantly, "Sex sells, Fleener; sex sells."

You know, what's amazing is that the guy keeps getting better—he works at it and his art continues to improve and evolve. That's what I call inspiring.

I'm glad that I've gotten to know both Crumb and his wife, Aline, a little bit over the years; however, hero worship is a hard monkey to kick. Crumb is simply too important, a fact I know that he plays down, but let's face it: in each era or generation there are those individuals who stand out and make waves on their own terms, and we admire them. John Lennon said he never would have picked up a guitar if not for Elvis Presley, and I wouldn't have had the zeal to draw underground comix if not for Robert Crumb, and I'm on a very, very long list.

D A M E   D A R C Y

Cartoonist: Meatcake

❚ can't remember a time when I didn't know about R. Crumb. In Idaho, my father and uncle played and taught me all kinds of bluegrass instruments, and were artists as well. Apparently, my uncle knew Robert Crumb when he lived in San Francisco in the sixties. How close they were, I cannot say, but as a child I saw copies of *Zap* and it showed me I could use comic books as a means for artistic expression without having to pander to the normal expectations that they should be cutesy or cheeseball superhero style.

I admire the way Mr. Crumb draws, his love for old things, and his taste in music. He's an introspective cynic, educated not only by books but by the school of hard knocks. He portrays situations and characters with a childlike timeless honesty, obsessing so minutely that at times he is overly analytical and self-consuming. But the end result even in this is funny.

Many women have called him sexist because of how he often

portrays females in his comics. I've been hurt by this also; but once I saw past the initial surface of it, I realized Robert Crumb is merely depicting and exposing the Id that all men share but few are able to put into concrete terms. Through doing this, he is not only laughing at women but also at the way men behave as well.

He is a visionary who has opened the door for an entirely new art form to emerge, somewhere between Tijuana Bibles and religious tracts.

If it weren't for R. Crumb and others like him, many current cartoonists of the younger generation would have an even harder time being recognized, let alone being published. And for this, I am eternally grateful. Viva le Crumb!

Artist, Critic, and Curator: The Museum of Modern Art

▌have my own stash. On the shelf in the corner of my studio. Old *Tintin*s, old *Mad*s, and a half-stack—like alien pancakes—of thin Crumb "comix." Except for the *Mad*s, which my friends and I traded back and forth until the staples pulled and the covers fell off, these vintage comic books are in mint condition. The fact is I never shared my *Tintin*s with anybody, or my Crumbs. They were private pleasures, and I guarded them jealously.

This hoarding was certainly not done out of shame. No, the reason I kept them to myself was that in their own very different way each occasioned all-absorbing fantasies and I had no tolerance for the reality-affirming distractions of stains, smudges, rips, or telltale signs of fevered reading.

Tintin transported me to exotic parts of the world; Crumb transported me to exotic parts of my own mind and gave me a mockingly vivid appreciation of my darker nature. Bracketing my adolescence, Herge and Crumb's images set themselves apart from my regular comic book fare, by virtue of the utter graphic clarity with which they depicted the things my thrill-hungry subconscious craved.

"Take a tip from R. Crumb," trumpets the header on the back cover of *Despair*, "Drawing Cartoons is Fun!" "And remember," reads the last line on the page, "It's Only Lines On Paper, Folks!!" Crumb's genius is to have made the lines with which he described America run amok so plain.

Contemporaneous psychedelic art was a zoomy version of nineteenth century symbolism; acid and amphetamines had replaced absinthe and opium as the mind-altering drugs of choice but the hallucinations they triggered ran to the same decorative excess. Crumb was much too down-to-earth about his obsessions to indulge in such mannerisms. Even his druggiest pictures are drawn with complete manual sobriety, as if he were reporting with iron-willed objectivity on the most extreme psychological states.

Crumb's thick unequivocal black line nevers races ahead of his scrutinizing vision in pursuit of pictorial hunches or special effects. No matter how deliciously monstrous the girl he depicts may be, for example, or how extreme the lust or anger she inspires in his various alter egos, Crumb's steady hand documents them all with unwavering authority. In a world of hop-headed hares, he was the tortoise who didn't miss a trick.

Crumb's triumph is that of the nerd who ended up having more fun than the cool kids—even if it was mostly in his head. But, that, after all, is where a whole generation wanted to be anyway, and many blew their circuits out trying to get to. Meanwhile, Crumb was there all along, chronicling their desperate attempts at inward escape and otherwise going about his id-crazed business with great, pitiless artistry. He's still at it. Strange to think that when my children raid my collection of Crumb comix, confident that they have found my guilty secret, they will in fact be sneaking off with the classics. I won't tip them off and spoil their discovery.

Cartoonist: The New Yorker, Steven

A few years ago, Crumb did a strip for *Premiere* about the Academy Awards. The magazine had sent him to attend the ceremony in Los Angeles to get his impressions, which were, as you can guess, horror and anxiety from being exposed to all the falseness and glamour of the Hollywood movie industry. To make a long story short, the last panel of his strip pictured him back home at last, reading a copy of my comic book, *Steven*. Needless to say, this made my day-week-year. To not be hated by Crumb is an honor for any cartoonist. I found it particularly surprising because when I first started my strip, I blatantly ripped him off, either thinking no one would see my stuff and call me on it, or hoping it would be taken as a homage to greatness. I just figured that was the way you did underground comix.

In 1971, when I was fifteen, I did a comic called *Crap* and the main story was about a teenager who goes out looking for "gurls," but ends up with a transvestite named Ralph. The other story was about greasers on motorcycles who go looking for "gurls" but wind up getting beaten up by their boyfriends and end up in jail after punching a cop. My style on the first story imitated *National Lampoon*'s M. K. Brown, and on the second it imitated that of the artists in *CARtoons*, which was my favorite magazine (besides *Car Model*). The concept and format, however, was clearly *Zap*-inspired. The only Crumb comics I owned back then—*Uneeda*, *Mr. Natural*, and *Motor City*—were given to me by a friend and were kept in my bedside table.

I would look at those early Crumbisms—with their alluring adolescent taboo subjects of tits 'n' ass, drugs 'n' booze, and violence 'n' sex, and I'd identify with the "coolness" of it the same way I would when I'd listen to Country Joe and the Fish and B. B. King when I should've been listening to the Archies and the 1910 Fruitgum Company. I knew there was something cool and dirty about it that I wanted to know more about.

Speaking of music, that strikes me as a good means of comparison to put Crumb in some sort of historical perspective, since the history of his brand of comics is only now being written. Crumb has had the same kind of influence on younger "underground" cartoonists that Chuck Berry or Little Richard had on rock musicians, or that Bill Monroe had on bluegrass players. That is to say, he practically created it. These musicians took styles that were already existing and distilled them to create something new and original.

Maybe it would be more flattering for Crumb to be compared to someone earlier, like Charlie Parker, Charlie Patton, or Charlie Pool. Sorry, Robert, that's about as far back as I go. But how about a poem:

He's a very good artist
Like Rembrandt Van Rijn
When he draws an ass
He does it with class
His stuff makes me cream

Cartoonist: The New York Times, Details, Time, Rolling Stone

The year: 1970. The place: Cleveland Heights, Ohio. "Open up! I understand you have comics in there." After a pause, Harvey Pekar buzzed me in. I was eleven or twelve years old at the time and felt it was my god-given right to be in contact with anyone who had comics. My best friend, Seth Tobocman, who was Harvey's paperboy, had tipped me off and I barged in. Harvey showed me a handful of old comics, but then he pulled out an original page he had stored in back with his hundreds of 78-rpm records. It was a beautiful hand-colored drawing of a guy pissing into a toilet, done by an old friend of his named Robert Crumb.

I had seen my first Crumb art the previous summer in a 'zine called *Promethean Enterprises* and was only just becoming familiar with his work. Mostly my tastes ran toward superheroes, but there was something wonderfully subversive about seeing a cartoon character's genitals.

Shortly after this, I stumbled upon a good-sized collection of 78-rpm records left in my parent's basement by the previous owner. I called Harvey, who, after going through them, told me his friend Crumb would probably be interested in trading artwork for some of them.

At this time, Seth and I had begun publishing a comics fanzine called *G.A.S. Lite* (The Official Magazine of the Cleveland Graphic Arts Society), so I asked Harvey if he would also send along an interview/questionnaire for Crumb to answer as part of the trade. A month or two later, Harvey called me to come pick up a package Crumb had mailed him. It included written responses to our questions and an original page from *Uneeda Comics*. I excitedly rode home on my bike, clutching the art and interview in my hand as it fluttered in the wind.

Crumb had answered the questionnaire succinctly, filling in the huge space we'd left after each question: To "Could you give us a brief rundown on the history of underground comix?" he wrote, "No." To "What were, or are, your goals in life?" he was more elaborate: "To draw as many comics as I possibly can without getting in a rut, and to fuck a lot of women and girls, and to listen to a lot of good music, and to take a lot of drugs and eat a lot ... eventually I hope to die ... but not right away."

After much difficulty, we found an adult willing to type these and the rest of his responses, which Seth and I published in 1971. Much to our surprise, that issue of *G.A.S. Lite* sold out of its entire hundred-copy print run.

In the spring of 1972, along with Robert Armstrong and Allan Dodge, Crumb passed through Cleveland and stayed at Harvey's apartment. One night the group of them paid me a visit to check out the 78-rpm records. After picking me up and "flying" me around my room a bit (I was small for my age) and dutifully sitting through tea and coffee cake with my parents, they picked through the records and found about fifty that caught their eye. It was agreed they could have them in exchange for drawings. Crumb, at my request, was

176

going to draw a guy "truckin' " and Robert Armstrong would do Mickey Rat, or something similar.

A couple of days later, I dropped by Harvey's to pick up the finished art, but Crumb hadn't begun working. To keep an antsy thirteen-year-old occupied while he hunched over a desk drawing up a storm, Crumb sat me on the couch and gave me his fat sketchbook filled with incredible doodles. To say I was ballsy at that age would be a gross understatement. As I sat pondering, it seemed to me that all those records were worth more than some drawing this Crumb guy could whip out. (I'm dying a thousand tiny deaths as I write this.) I mean, it wasn't like he drew Spiderman or anything. So I asked if he would throw a page from his sketchbook into the deal. *No?* Well, then how about letting me photocopy some pages and print them? Crumb agreed, simply handed over his sketchbook and let me ride off on my bike to the public library copy machine.

About six months later, I published the first of two hand-assembled 'zines collecting these sketches and the interview under the title *Melotoons*. At around this same time, I began to see Crumb in a different light. This was not just the result of receiving letters from rabid Crumb fans who ordered the 'zine—it was also thanks to my older sister's boyfriend who let me read the comics I had been prohibited by law from purchasing. Coincidentally, around this time (age fourteen to fifteen), I began experimenting with drugs and I found a sudden awareness of the vast well of humor and insight (not to mention appreciation of the sexual content) in Crumb's comics.

By the time I published *Melotoons* #2, at the age of sixteen, I was comparing Crumb to the Beatles in terms of artistic importance, now a full-fledged rabid enthusiast. It did leak into my subconscious, however, that there may have been something unbalanced in our records-for-art trade. With this nagging thought, I abandoned *Melotoons* and threw out the remaining copies.

Since then, Harvey Pekar went on to publish *American Splendor*, and Crumb, based no doubt on our traumatic encounter, went on to create the strip

"When the Goddamn Jews Take Over America!" I've long since resigned from Z.O.G. (Zionist Occupation Government) and as penance, have become a cartoonist and allowed myself to be exploited by a long list of publishers.

The last time I saw Crumb was in France at the Angoulême Comics Expo in 1992. When I spoke to him briefly, he warmed my heart by telling me he still had, and cherished, one or two of the records from our ancient trade. A bit later, I was just approaching him when he suddenly mounted (with permission, in trade for a drawing) the woman in front of him, and rode her around the convention aisles.

I forget what I had wanted to say to him, but I was reminded of his closing remarks from our 1971 interview: "Well, in conclusion I would just like to say that I don't think you guys oughta take comic books so seriously. I mean, dig on 'em, look at 'em, swap 'em, trade 'em, collect 'em, but don't take them so *goddamn* seriously. Comic and science-fiction fans of the world, get laid!!"

R A Y   Z O N E

Publisher/Writer: The 3-D Zone

Like many great artists, Crumb creates out of an inner necessity, a compulsion that has produced a prodigious amount of work and continues to do so. It may well be that by the year 2000, one of the most highly regarded artists of the late twentieth-century will be R. Crumb. Yet it is not his overwhelmingly accomplished technique that distinguishes him, but his symphonic use of representation and narrative at the service of a larger cause, vision and, sometimes, demon. That purpose is *satire* and it is the immense specific scope of his satire that distinguishes him. This is satire that demolishes not only the puny pretensions of the individual but also those of time, history, and society. The satire of Crumb demolishes *all* that stands before it. It is an immense affront to, and simultaneous sweeping away of, the lies of history and the hypocrisy of culture in which are woven the insidious and blood-red strands of sex, religion, identity, nationalism, gender, and class. This cleansing and devastating act of washing away the accumulated lies of civilization is the healthiest act of preparation to build a new, millennial society founded upon the values of humanity rather than technology; spirit rather than politics.

Let's consider Crumb's technique: the look of his art, his line, his cross-hatch and stipple, his use of light and shadow. There is more pure American drive, a stylistic amalgam of populist energy, in a single Crumb cartoon than in all of the products combined from the Pop Art movement of the sixties. Crumb's lines are inherently about the New World, folks; the gleaming and profuse energy of lowbrow America.

Crumb's immense libido has been cruelly (yet fortunately for us) tied to a most unprepossessing physiognomy and his cartoon art is his revenge against every macho asshole or beautiful female bitch who has insulted him. That immense genius, driven by native sexual energy, will have its day on paper in lines that assault, excoriate, and ultimately devastate all that have stood before it without respect, all that have not honored the humble figure which masks the towering intellect reposing in the ultrasensitive shell.

Consider for a moment Crumb's dedication to his craft, the pure workmanship in what he does. With his ever-present sketchbook, he records whatever is about him. His portraits of American musicians and everyday people are loving linear vessels that contain humanity and pathos. Crumb's narratives embody the very definition of "freedom of thought." His mind and pen wander absolutely at large in the known and unknown universe. It is a cosmos insultingly white—blank—until he invests that page of paper with some of the most meaningful lines and squiggles that we have in all of art history. Yet his work transcends mere art and penetrates to the very heart of human experience. It captures the fright and beauty of a querulous and sensitive consciousness adrift, both powerless and immortal, in a brash and ultimately venal universe. But that squalid realm is transfigured by the sensitive hand of the cartoonist that invests meaning into the cruelly chaotic spectacle.

180

Filmmaker: Dead Man, Stranger than Paradise, Down by Law

Back in the mid-to-late-seventies, when I was a student at Columbia College, I wrote a paper for a course called "Contemporary Civilization," or something like that. Anyway, the subject of my paper was the work of R. Crumb, and after reading it the professor (whose name I don't recall) called me in for an appointment. He informed me that he had no choice but to give me an incomplete for the course because the subject of my writing was unacceptable. I really don't remember anything about the paper itself—most likely it contained comparisons of Crumb to the likes of William Hogarth, George Grosz, Max Fleischer, et cetera—but I do recall the professor telling me that, although my paper was "interesting," a "contemporary cartoonist" was not the proper focus for the course. I don't remember if I argued with him or just walked out like a zombie, but I imagine that I probably had thoughts along the lines of: "Shit. I *know* he's not gonna accept something on Albert Ayler or the MC5.

I guess he wants something on Roy Lichtenstein or Le Corbusier ... Oh well, fuck it."

Now, twenty-plus years later and looking back, I realize I had every right to kick that professor's ass. Hogarth, Grosz, the Fleischer brothers, Tex Avery, Charles Addams, et cetera *are* great artists. And so is R. Crumb. In certain ways, he may even be the greatest of them all. But hell, this isn't some contest, or some damn awards ceremony. This is just my opinion. The editor of this book asked for it, so there it is. R. Crumb is an original. He's a great cartoonist, and that, in my book, deserves great respect. Our "contemporary civilization" is lucky to have him, and to have his work.